A Family Year Abroad:
How to Live
Outside the Borders

By
Chris Westphal

Great Potential Press, Inc.
(formerly Gifted Psychology Press, Inc.)
P.O. Box 5057
Scottsdale, AZ 85261
www.giftedbooks.com

A Family Year Abroad: How to Live Outside the Borders

Cover Design/Layout: ATG Productions, Inc.
Interior Design/Layout: Spring Winnette

Published by
Great Potential Press, Inc.
(formerly Gifted Psychology Press, Inc.)
P.O. Box 5057
Scottsdale, AZ 85261
www.giftedbooks.com

Printed and bound in the United States of America.
05 04 03 02 01   6 5 4 3 2 1

Library of Congress Cataloging-in-Publication Data
Westphal, Chris, 1953-
    A Family Year Abroad: How to Live Outside the Borders / by
Chris Westphal.
        p. c.m
    Includes index.
    ISBN 0-910707-47-2
        1. Prague (Czech Republic)--Description and travel. 2. Americans--Foreign
countries--Handbooks, manuals, etc. 3. Americans--Czech Republic--Prague. 4.
Westphal, Chris, 1953- I. Title.
DB2614.W47 2001
943.71'2--dc21   2001033227

ISBN: 0-910707-47-2

DEDICATION

This book is dedicated
to my wife, Stephanie,
and to my children, Drew and Kelsey.
Without them, any adventure,
no matter how bold,
would be without meaning.

Whatever you can do or dream you can, begin it. Boldness has genius, power, and magic in it.

—Johann Wolfgang Von Goethe

A Family Year Abroad:

HOW TO LIVE OUTSIDE THE BORDERS

What's wrong with this picture? We're moving to a country we've never even visited. We embark with high expectations, minimal plans, and lots of romance. So the question really is, what's right with this picture?

Evaluating different countries as to their suitability for one's family. Resources to consider when starting the initial planning process.

How to make preliminary plans for expatriate living, including deciding whether to sell, rent, or leave your house vacant, and tips on how to do so with minimal risk.

Hobnobbing with the Foreign Police

What to bring and what not to bring for the early part of your trip, including over-the-counter medications. What to consider regarding computers and electrical equipment.

Who Put the Klutz in Kludsky?

Travel is broadening in its own right, but unless you're devoted to home-schooling, you'll probably want your school-aged children in some sort of school program. Here's what to think about when considering various options for educating your children while you live abroad. And have you considered getting a graduate degree while abroad? Distance learning programs make it possible.

Use the Good China

What to look out for and what to do when you realize you're not in Kansas anymore.

'Carp' Diem

How to find a place to live—things to consider, things to avoid.

How to set up your life back in the States so that it will run easily while you're away. Managing money via electronic banking, automatic bill payment, and wire transfers.

Health concerns while living abroad. Health insurance and medical care considerations while abroad. Notes about other types of insurance to think about for your family. Information on how to rent a car, how to bring your car with you, and auto insurance considerations.

Some basic steps to setting up a Web site.

Traveling with children can be a chore—or not. Here are some ways to make everyone's life easier while on the road.

The Long Road Back

In the beginning, a year seemed like an eternity. Near the end, it seemed too short.

I Said Goodbye, You Say Hello

In some ways, coming back home is more difficult than settling into a new country. What to look out for, and how to cope.

I Do Declare! I Have Nothing to Declare

U.S. Customs rules, and tips and ideas about shipping.

Expat Light: House Exchanges

If living abroad for a year or more is impractical for your family, house exchanges offer a non-touristy opportunity to experience another country.

A Host of Student Exchange Programs

If an extended period abroad is impossible for the whole family, your child may be interested in spending a semester, six months, or a year abroad living with a host family. Or you may want to invite a foreign student to live with your family.

Your Bags Are Packed, Your Days Are Numbered

For the order-minded reader, here are lists of what to do and when to do it to make your departure and your return go as smoothly as possible.

It's All in the Web... Somewhere

Listings of Web sites highlighted in this book.

PREFACE

About This Book... and More

This book is a hybrid: part narrative of our family's year living in Prague, Czech Republic; part instruction manual for individuals and families considering, or in the midst of, spending an extended period outside of the borders of their own country.

Though living abroad is hardly unusual—according to the U.S. State Department, almost four million Americans live outside of the country—our family did it in an unusual way. We went entirely on our own, without the benefit of a corporation or a government paying our way or solving our problems. We learned a lot of lessons by doing it that way, and that's the reason for this book.

We learned that moving abroad for a year or longer is a process that will impact every area of your life. Work, school, daily routines, friendships, cultural perspectives, and anything else you can name will change on the day you board that plane and head overseas. There will be novelty, excitement, and adventure, and there will also be loneliness, confusion, and periods of time when you wonder what possessed you to do something so bold.

The narrative portions in each chapter of this book provide a look at our lives abroad as we discovered and re-discovered who we were as a family and re-defined ourselves in relation to the adventure we had undertaken together. Also contained in those portions are a series of e-mail messages, mostly concerning my novel, *Echo Valley,* (HMR, 1997) which was published just days before we left for Prague. The saga of *Echo Valley* was an important element in my life abroad, and these messages—mostly between my publisher and me—comprise an absurd, and at the time, often maddening story-within-a-story.

Each chapter also offers tips, resources, and practical advice on everything from finding a school for your children, to maintaining your finances, to keeping up with friends back home.

I relied on our family's experiences in writing this book and also on the experiences of dozens of other expatriates. While abroad, we met many families who had lived outside of the U.S. for years, and they were kind enough to offer their advice and insight during my research.

Through various expatriate portal Web sites and message boards, I also contacted expatriates all over the world. Many of them filled out an Internet-based questionnaire, and I used their quotes and answers throughout. I also searched the Internet extensively and found helpful sites and resources that can make many aspects of life abroad go more easily.

Many things are important when you live abroad, but some of the most important ones can't be packed in a suitcase. They are experience, wisdom, and humor. I've done my best to put all three into the pages that follow.

–Chris Westphal

INTRODUCTION

Living Outside the Borders

This photo, taken by a flight attendant aboard the Virgin Atlantic flight from Los Angeles to London, shows my family as we left to live for a year abroad in Prague.

I admit to a cheerful, though somewhat unfocused, expression. Maybe it's just the Valium kicking in. My daughter, Kelsey, age 7, wears a black baseball cap backwards and sleek sunglasses; she looks too cool for this crowd. My 10-year-old son, Drew, sits like a judge, hands folded on the seat tray, as though he has heard all the evidence already and is saying, "All right, you've presented your case about this Prague idea. But you haven't proven that it's a good idea." My wife, Stephanie, sits farthest from the camera, hardly reached by the flash. She smiles openly and is probably just as zoned out as I am, but her disorientation has more to do with simpler, maternal things, such as: "We have no home. What are we going to do for a year in a foreign city where we don't even have an apartment?"

The photograph shows my family before we left for Prague, but it was also before a lot of other things, too. The photo shows us before we all had, in one way or another, fallen apart and been put back together again by the familial gravitational forces that were the most important component of that amazing year.

Why Prague?

Neither Stephanie nor I had ever been to the Czech Republic, and we have no Czech ancestry. So it's reasonable to ask, "Why Prague?" At the time the photo was taken, we could have presented a thousand convincing reasons. We might have mentioned the country's long and interesting history, which is, in many ways, the history of central Europe. We might have alluded to the Czech Republic's literary heritage, or Prague's splendid architecture, it being the only major European city not flattened in World War II. Or we could have offered the Czech Republic's tumult and excitement as it emerged from 40-plus years of communism, or the reported low cost of living, or the country's tradition of brewing fine beer.

All of these things were true, of course. Especially the beer.

But the larger question was, "Why go at all?" And the answer to that was harder to pin down.

One friend described it as "the most creative mid-life crisis I've ever heard of." If it were simply that, we wouldn't be the only American family we met to move to Prague independently—that is, without having ethnic ties, relatives, or a corporation or government willing to pay our way.

Even people who had spent years abroad with their families were amazed that we had tackled the entire enterprise on our own. They, too, asked the simple question, "Why?" By then, we had formulated a few stock answers:

A) For romance and adventure.
B) Because it'll be great for the kids.
C) Because we really meant to do this kind of thing in our twenties, but we forgot.
D) Because we were in a rut, and we didn't want it to get any deeper.
E) Why not?

They were all true. But early on, "Why not?" seemed to be the most honest answer. In hindsight, I see even more reasons.

I see now how living abroad brought us closer together because we depended so much more on one another. It provided our children with a glimpse of the world and the people in it. They appreciate that world now and ultimately have a better understanding of their place in it and of the opportunities it offers.

We arrived in Prague with 12 suitcases—four of them little carry-ons roughly large enough to hold a toothbrush and pair of socks. We left Prague knowing what it feels like to embark on something bold and unknown and to succeed at it. That's something that we'll always have. In the final analysis, just the knowledge that we can do something entirely different with our lives made the journey worthwhile.

Dreams Delayed Are Dreams Denied

As children, we believe that everything is possible—even those things that are impossible. Then we find out that we really don't disappear when we hide behind our hands, and we don't become Superman just because we wear a cape. I'm still coping with that bitter truth.

But life is, in a way, bitter truth; through education and work and relationships, we learn limits. Often, we surrender our dreams.

Especially if we're successful, it is easy to settle into complacency—to define ourselves in terms of our profession or our accomplishments or our children (to which I plead guilty, guilty, guilty!) and to forget that there may be an entirely new way of living that we just forgot to dream about.

For Stephanie and me, travel has always provided a vital spark of adventure, but outside of a three week stay in Paris when Drew was just a year old, we had seldom traveled outside of California, let alone gone abroad. But the children were getting older, and we were getting more restless. Maybe this was a mid-life crisis, or maybe it was the honest realization that life doesn't last forever; that cherished dreams can die a quiet death.

We embarked on this grand adventure with idealistic zeal, and it felt wonderful to tackle something wholly new. Having children, of course, added a multitude of considerations to the process and also gave it far more meaning. Most importantly, we believed that the children would learn by our example that new experience and, by extension, life itself is there to be embraced. For all of their conscious lives, they had lived in a small Southern California town. Despite all its virtues and comforts, we didn't want them to believe, however unconsciously, that the world begins and ends at the city limits. We believed that the experience of living in another country would greatly expand their view of the world and of their place in it.

Stephanie and I began planning our year abroad 12 months prior to our departure. Stephanie learned that she could teach English as a

Second Language there and finally complete her teaching credential program, which she had started years earlier at U.C. Berkeley. This made a lot of sense, as her status as a teacher would also allow us to apply for resident status. I've always worked as a writer, but for years had struggled to break into television. After zig-zagging through stints as a journalist and a corporate communications writer, I (and a writing partner) worked as story editors on a network comedy. But toward the end of our contract on the show, my partner announced that she was going out on her own. This was a devastating blow to me, but she was resolute.

Stephanie and I then moved to the slower-paced—and more affordable—city of Ojai, where I began writing novels, while also doing corporate communications and other writing on a freelance basis for various clients. I was diligent, focused, and prolific; in five years, I'd completed four novels. I was also unsuccessful in selling any of them. So as we prepared to leave for Prague, I was at a seeming crossroads: should I continue writing fiction, or try to get a full-time position writing public relations or corporate communications?

With my two major corporate communications clients, I knew I would be able to work over the Internet while in Prague. I also hoped to get work with clients there, but was worried that I might miss a terrific opportunity in the U.S. because I was out of the country. It was a risk I was more than willing to take. We were fortunate to have a modest income from a rental property that we owned with partners, and also a portfolio of investments that we had purchased with money from the estate of my father, who had died in 1984. It had sputtered along for years, but in the mid-90s, it was skyrocketing in value.

Though we knew we would probably have to dip into savings to get through the year, the timing seemed perfect. Naturally, this financial cushion made things easier for us. However, in today's global economy, opportunities exist that make living abroad feasible for many families. Most large companies have overseas offices, and thanks to the Internet, independent consultants can set up shop anywhere in the world. Flexibility in how you work and in how you adapt to changes in your life is a key asset for a rewarding experience abroad.

Our children didn't really see it that way, though. In fact, when we first mentioned the idea of moving to Prague to Drew and Kelsey, they didn't believe we *were* serious. As plans progressed and they realized that we were serious, they were resistant to going. Fortunately, neither had entered that dreaded period of adolescence when their social sphere becomes more important than anything else, or when they can mount a serious rebellion. To them, a year still seemed like an eternity, and we listened to their concerns—mostly about missing friends—and assured them as well as we could. But we also knew that all of our lives would change. Despite the positive benefits that we anticipated, there was no question that all of us would sacrifice things—perhaps important things—by going. Stephanie was particularly concerned that friendships she had forged in our four years in Ojai would weaken in our absence.

Still, the adventure was too tantalizing to abandon. We did everything we could think of to generate enthusiasm, stopping short of presenting it all as a very long vacation. We watched Czech movies (including the Academy Award winner *Kolja*), learned a bit of the language together through a set of tapes, learned about the country as much as we could, and generally reassured the children that their friends would still like them when they returned home.

Outside the Borders

Both Stephanie and I spent considerable mental energy playing out various disaster scenarios: dread diseases, plane crashes, terrorist bombings. The chances of something catastrophic happening were minimal, of course, but cataclysmic fantasies are just one of the prices that one pays for an active imagination. There was a plus side to imagination, too: it kept us going as the planning process continued. By going to Prague, we were re-imagining our world into something that fit us better. We wanted to be shaken and stirred. While I hoped I might be able to sell a book about the experience, I would have felt it worthwhile for its own sake, too—for the pure exhilaration of the new. Our year abroad as "freelance expatriates[1]" was our family's declaration that we wouldn't succumb to routine, no matter how comfortable it was. Uncertainty was part of the thrill.

So in the end, there was a much greater answer to the question of "Why?" than simply "Why not?" Although during our year abroad we often wondered what we had gotten ourselves into, on reflection, we wouldn't have done it any other way.

In that year, Stephanie and I rediscovered important elements of our own lives. Our children discovered new things about themselves. We're still making these discoveries more than two years after our return. I hope we continue to do so.

---

[1] There are, of course, politically motivated expatriates who leave the U.S., burn their passports, and renounce their citizenship. However, the overwhelming majority of expatriates are people whose professions or interests compel them to live outside their country.

But the four people in this photograph don't know that yet. Neither could they know the scope—or the fragility—of the idealism that had put them on this airplane at this time with this destination.

We were leaving our country and would live for a year in another country that we'd never even visited. We had leased our house, stored our furniture, and transferred our bank accounts into the name of our accountant, so returning to America in less than a year was virtually impossible—quitting wasn't an option for us.

The family in this photograph, this four of "us back then" who look at me now from behind a clear plastic sheet in our photo album, then only knew a buzzing sense of adventure and uncertainty. They were too focused on their exhaustion from preparation and the hollow sense of loss that accompanied saying goodbye to friends. They had no idea what would transpire in the upcoming year, because they are confined to this picture. It would take until now for them to look back at this photo and see what lies outside its borders.

Ojai, California, April 2001

ONE

It Must Be a British Thing

"You know you're an expat when... you don't know the language and you are helpless to make the simplest communication."

—Michael Paprok, Prague

Our plan to move to Prague was well underway when serendipity struck. Through Barbara, a writer friend, I was put in contact with Terry Harris, an English publisher with the audacious plan to publish American first novels in England. For more than two years, I had struggled unsuccessfully to find a publisher for *Echo Valley*, the first of my planned trilogy of comic novels. By the time I had contacted Terry Harris, I was pretty disillusioned by the whole publishing business and figured that this unconventional route was worth a try. Wouldn't it be perfect, I imagined, to have the book published just prior to our departure? Not only would it be a great personal accomplishment, but it would give me an opportunity while in Europe to try and sell publication rights to other European publishers.

In January, I e-mailed Terry Harris the manuscript, and within days—record time for a publisher to respond; generally it takes months—he expressed strong interest. In February, he said he wanted to publish it, but first wanted to meet me face-to-face. He would be in New York in March. Could I arrange to see him then?

Barbara had received the same request and had driven in from Connecticut. But I would have to fly in from California. "He says he never publishes anyone he hasn't met," Barbara said. "It must be a British thing."

MORE DATA, PLEASE... According to the U.S. Department of State, some 3,784,693 Americans live abroad. If you're in Germany, you'll have 200,000 Americans keeping you company. If you're in Guinea-Bissau, only 25.

ACCORDING TO THE EXPERTS... CHILDREN WHO LEARN A FOREIGN LANGUAGE PRIOR TO THE AGE OF 13 CAN MORE EASILY DO SO WITHOUT AN ACCENT DUE TO NEUROLOGICAL AND PHYSICAL CHARACTERISTICS THAT CHANGE AT PUBERTY.

MORE DATA, PLEASE... The Central Intelligence Agency isn't just a club for guys who like to wear trench coats. They've compiled a huge database called *The World Factbook*, which has maps, histories, and exhaustive data about almost everywhere on earth. On the World Wide Web, the *Factbook* is located at www.odci.gov/cia/publications/factbook/index.html.

That was good enough for me. Besides, the flight was only a few hundred dollars, so what did I have to lose—other than, well, a few hundred dollars?

A couple of weeks later, I waited in the gloomy lobby of a small midtown Manhattan hotel. I got the distinct impression that rooms were let by the month and that the rent was paid in cash.

I buzzed Terry's room, and a few moments later I was in his small suite. Tall and wiry, Terry spoke with what any regular viewer of Masterpiece Theater would recognize as a workingman's accent. By way of introduction, he explained that he had been an agent in London for 10 years, then moved into publishing when he bought a small company that was in bankruptcy. His having been an agent could explain the streetwise aura that he projected. After all, some literary agents are hustlers at heart and do whatever they can to get the deal made.

I took a seat on a slumping sofa across from a row of books propped on a nicked table. "These are a few of the titles we've done," said Terry nonchalantly.

The books occupied every conceivable genre, ranging from historical fiction, to fat coffee table books loaded with color photos, to a novel based on the true-life adventures of a World War I RAF pilot. There was even a series on obscure commercial transport vehicles used in England year-by-year.

In addition to his evident track record, Terry had a marketing wrinkle that sounded reasonably viable and also appealed to my romanticism. "We're an English company publishing American first novels—overturning the corporate domination of publishing." Having been turned down several times by the corporate publishing world, this idea appealed to me.

As he warmed to his pitch, Terry paced about the room. He spoke with the fervor of a revolutionary, seemingly gathering energy from the worn carpet and faded paint. "First novels are by far the riskiest area of publishing," he said. "But any real publisher loves to bring them out, because that's where the new talent comes from. And I love writers. I love discovering new talent and bringing it to the world. And your book will be the first one under our new imprint."

Dealing with Terry Harris was an entirely new experience. He introduced me to the dowdy Caroline, "my editor for the past 15 years, and one of the best in the business!" and to the young and frazzled Charles Roberts, "my business partner and a top marketing man. How did it go with Harper and Row?"

"Fine," said Charles through tight lips. "Pleased to meet you," he said to me. Then, hefting a bulging briefcase, he was off.

Previous to this meeting, all of my discussions with Terry had been over the Internet. I had no idea why he wanted to meet me, other than to judge whether my picture would look good on the dust jacket. I wanted to meet him to see if he was legitimate, though I had checked him out as best I could over the Internet and found nothing amiss.

But still... wasn't there something odd about a publisher who responded so quickly? I thought publishers delighted in keeping potential authors waiting. He said he had drawn up a contract, but did he expect me to pay for printing or something? Did he have a secret agenda, or was I just too cynical?

Those questions were in the forefront of my mind as Terry talked for perhaps an hour. He had little interest in my suggestions for generating domestic interest in my book. "We need to put some things in place before we reach that point," he said curtly.

MORE DATA, PLEASE... Council Travel is on the Web at www.ciee.org. Click on "Travel." To use Council Travel, you have to prove you're a teacher or student and purchase an identity card from them for $22. Council Travel, 205 E. 42nd Street, New York, NY 10017, Tel: 800.226.8624

Discount airfares, hotel accommodations, and rental cars are also available through Cheap Tickets, Inc., on the Web at www.cheaptickets.com.

TIP: Many companies offer discounted airfares. Try a Web search using *discount international airline travel* or *flight consolidators* to get an idea of available discount airfares.

MORE DATA, PLEASE... If your pet would also like to spend some time abroad, take a look at the U.S. Department of Agriculture's information for traveling with pets at www.usda.gov.

MORE DATA, PLEASE... Airline safety data and information is available on the Web at www.airsafe.com.

From time to time, he'd reach for one of the books and tell me which award it had won or which glowing review it had received. He outlined an ambitious publicity plan for *Echo Valley* and alluded to various film producers he dealt with who were eager to review the manuscript. I remained cautiously skeptical—always a good stance for me to take with anyone making promises.

But when he showed me a photo of the grand English countryside estate he was renovating, which belonged in a BBC costume drama, I thought that finally I understood this man: Terry Harris was a publisher in the eccentric British tradition, right out of a P. G. Wodehouse novel. He apparently had a large fortune somewhere (witness the house) and was the type who defied tradition, forsaking convention for the sake of something he believed in—even when everyone else said he was insane.

A British publisher was ideal for me, because *Echo Valley* was, after all, a satire, and the British have a long tradition of publishing those. I let myself start getting excited. Why, with the right promotion, good reviews in the right places, a foreign sale or two... and it would make a great movie....

It was nearing lunchtime. Terry said he had a meeting with a "prospective American partner."

"You mentioned a contract," I said. "Can I take a look at it?"

Terry slapped his forehead, went into the adjoining room where Caroline was talking on the phone, and emerged with a four-page contract. "We do want to get moving on this right away," he said tentatively.

"I'll look it over now," I said.

In a bagel shop a few blocks away, I read the contract, which was clear and reasonable. Terry would pay a small advance against royalties—a third of it on signing. He would get a percentage of other rights, but the majority were mine. Basically, this was a good deal, and I was pleased.

Returning to his suite an hour or so later, I asked a few more questions, got satisfactory answers, and handed over the signed document. Terry smiled and quickly wrote out a check to me.

That evening, I called home. "He seems on the level," I told Stephanie, "contract and everything." She offered her enthusiastic congratulations, but then added, " It does still seem a little fast, doesn't it?"

I admitted that it did, but countered with, "He gave me a check. What can I say?" In our relationship, I am the impulsive one and Stephanie is the careful one. It's a dynamic that's probably saved me from disaster more often than not and propelled her into some interesting and fulfilling adventures, too. I could understand her skepticism; I had had my hopes raised and dashed dozens of times over the past few years, though, and I desperately wanted this one to pan out.

Flying home, I couldn't help but reflect on how easily this had gone—and wonder whether I had been taken in by an elaborate scam. But what, exactly, was the scam? *He* had paid *me,* so he was losing money from the start. He hadn't asked for any money—and he never did. What kind of an idiot publishes first novels, which are notoriously difficult to turn a profit on even if they're acquired for free? If Terry Harris was operating a scam, it was the most cockeyed scam ever conceived.

Just four months later—no time at all in publishing, where books typically take nine months to a year from acquisition to publication— *Echo Valley* was published in hardback and had a beautiful full-color dust jacket designed by Charles Roberts, who besides being a "top marketing man," as Terry had boasted, was also a graphic illustrator of considerable talent.

Soon after the publication, I was invited to a local bookstore to do a reading. On the bookstore's airy patio, Stephanie, Drew and Kelsey, my mother, several aunts and uncles, plus friends were in the audience. The reading went perfectly, and the store sold some 40 of the 60 books they had on hand.

"That's the best we've ever done at a reading," the manager told me.

I happily abandoned my skepticism. "You have to admit it's come out all right," I told Stephanie, a little too confidently.

To my amazement and delight, Terry Harris' plan for his publishing house was working out just as he had outlined it. Since we had met, he

```
Subject: Re: Question
Date: Fri, 24 Jul 1997 15:04:14
From: Chris Westphal
To: Terry Harris

Dear Terry,
The woman I'm dealing with in Prague speaks perfect
English, has a good sense of humor, and is involved in
organizing the Carlsbad film festival; i.e., she's got
good connections and sensibilities. I think I'll ask
her to help as an "agent" with selling Echo Valley in
the Czech Republic, and wonder if you'd like me to
give her your catalog with an eye toward repping your
company in Central Europe. Are you interested? Her
name is Eva Kacerová². Let me know, and I'll discuss it
with her.
-CRW
```

---

[2] In Czech, the suffix "ova" is added to the surnames of all women. Eva's husband's surname is Kacer.

had already acquired three more novels and planned to open a New York office. About my book, he said during a phone conversation, "I'm going to go all the way with this—really make a splash."

I was pleased to actually have my book in hand now, because we were scheduled to leave for Prague in two days. In addition to setting up freelance jobs in Prague, I would also bring copies along and try to sell European rights. A sale to a foreign language publisher would mean not only income, but would increase the chance that ultimately a movie sale could be made. Whatever cosmic forces governed my professional life, they seemed to be aligning, at last, in my favor. Our move to Europe coincided with Terry Harris' move to New York; we would work both sides of the Atlantic. I couldn't see anything but good coming of the arrangement.

```
Subject: Re: Question
Date: Fri, 25 Jul 1997 09:22:29
From: Terry Harris
To: Chris Westphal

Dear Chris,
This is very kind of you. I am always very careful in
selecting or appointing an agent of any sort. A wrong
choice can do untold damage and whilst I am not ques-
tioning your judgment, I really do need some direct
contact and a little more information before making
these sort of major commitments. I have to answer to
my board of directors and, of course, the stockhold-
ers. Please pass on any info you have and I may well
be able to give you the OK very quickly. Thanks for
the help; don't let this message deter you!
Regards,
Terry
```

As we made our final arrangements for our year abroad and completed the seemingly endless task of packing, I would periodically be swept away by sweet and elaborate fantasies about our new life abroad: taking the family on a weekend trip to Germany or Austria or France and meeting European editors in lively outdoor cafes, where, owing to the unseasonably hot weather, we would drink Compari and soda; fielding phone calls from fascinated American newspaper writers who would be intrigued that The Novelist was off on the continent with his family while his book climbed the bestseller list; making a swift hop to England for the British launch; glancing out in the audience and spotting the novelist Martin Amis, who just dropped by to get a look at the competition.

At last, I was glimpsing a light at the end of the tunnel.

It was a train, headed straight toward me.

```
Subject: Re: Question
Date: Mon, 28 July 1997 15:22:02
From: Chris Westphal
To: Terry Harris

Terry,
I will mention it to her. I only know her by tele-
phone, and by how helpful she's been. I'll scope her
out and put her in touch with you or with Charles.
I'll know better once we're there! We're living in
boxes and suitcases right now; the house is complete-
ly a shambles. Movers, carpet cleaners... oy. I will
call Charles tomorrow re: going up to Worcestershire
during our visit.
-crw
```

Decisions, Decisions

As a college student, I was in a near fatal car accident. It wasn't my fault, and I received a small insurance settlement. The first thing I did was book a trip East Africa with my university. One of the women on the tour—a retired teacher—said that she had always wanted to visit Zanzibar. "I don't know what it is," she said, "but I've wanted to go since I was a little girl and I heard the name Zanzibar." When we visited Tanzania, she and some others made private arrangements and spent a weekend in Zanzibar.

I admired her a lot for having fulfilled her dream—almost enough to overlook the ridiculous safari suit she'd bought in Nairobi.

Weighing the Options

Finding a destination is as easy, and as difficult, as doing anything that you've long wanted to do. For us, the genesis of going to Prague was the televised 1989 demonstrations on Vaclavske Namesti (though we couldn't have pronounced the name then), when hundreds of thousands of people shook keys at the disgraced communist leaders as a gesture of dismissal.

We considered other cities before choosing Prague, but overall, Prague won for its history, its architecture, its location, and the fact that no one else we knew had ever been there. Those were things that were important to us and what we thought would make the experience more meaningful and enjoyable for our children.

You could choose a destination based on anything, but here are a few things to consider:

History: Take a look at any strip mall in the United States and imagine what it would be like to live there. Sure, the air-conditioning works and there are things to buy, but there isn't any history to make the place come alive and to share with your children.

Politics: I once visited the Seychelles just after a coup d'état. Machine gun-wielding teenagers guarded every intersection. Unless you're intrigued by the concept of you or your family being taken hostage, steer clear of politically unstable places.

Geography: You'll probably want to travel, and often only for a weekend. What's the neighborhood like, geographically speaking?

Language: This was one major drawback in Prague. The chance to learn another language is a major enticement to living abroad—and the more useful the language, the better. French, German, Spanish, Japanese; they're all great. Even Italian, if only because you could have such a good time at Italian restaurants back home. Czech? A beautiful language, but not exactly heard on every corner.

Schools: Your children may be able to attend local schools free of charge. They'll learn the language, make local friends, and be able to talk with them right in front of you and you'll have no idea what they're saying. There are also other school choices, including American Schools. (See Chapter Four for further information.)

Cost of living: In Prague, our U.S. dollars went a long way. In Paris, we would've lasted about three months.

But expense is far from the only thing you should take into consideration. Think also about things such as your family's ethnic heritage, food, a particular cultural interest, or a particular historical interest. In Prague, we became good friends with a Lutheran Pastor, Jim Krikava, who was an expert on the Reformation. Many of the notable events of that period occurred in Prague.

Expat Answers: *What are things to avoid when picking a country to live in?*

- *places where the locals are cautious around foreigners*
- *anyplace where you must live in an expat compound*
- *lack of opportunities beyond the first posting*
- *lack of goods from home*
- *places without some connection to home (i.e., international schools)*
- *politically dangerous locations*
- *places you never wanted to go*
- *countries with bad economies (you can never leave)*
- *anything too familiar*
- *negative attitudes toward women*
- *preconceived notions*
- *other people's opinions about your plan*
- *WAR*
- *thinking it will be easy*
- *thinking you will have all you have in your home country*
- *absence of human rights*
- *lack of public services*
- *cold weather, high taxes, and darkness*

–Various respondents

Flights of Fancy

International airfares vary wildly, depending on time of travel, length of stay, and popularity of the destination. Because Stephanie worked as a teacher, we used Council Travel, a flight consolidator that buys blocks of tickets from airlines, then sells them at a discount to teachers and to students.

One-way tickets are often ridiculously overpriced by the airlines to discourage one-way travel. Depending on the country of destination, you may have to show a return ticket in order to get a visa.

As our return date was uncertain, we purchased one-way tickets to Prague via London and found them at a very reasonable price. Our decision was partly an economic matter, too; we didn't want to let the airline play with several thousand dollars for a year when we could find a good use for it ourselves.

This turned out to be a false economy, because by the time we began shopping for return tickets—four months prior to our return—the deeply discounted fares were unavailable. Even if you plan to spend more than a year abroad, if you can book a one-year open-ended return, it's probably a good idea. Just use the return ticket for a visit back home.

TWO

A Ramblin' Kind of Family

"You know you're an expat when... even the fruit looks foreign."
-Lynn Gudhus, Japan

Just out of college, I took a job writing and editing a weekly newspaper in Mammoth Lakes, a little ski resort town in the Eastern Sierra. The newspaper publisher, Todd Watkins, had huge bushy eyebrows that seemed to function independently of any of his other facial features, and he liked to consider himself an authority on practically everything.

One of the few perquisites of my job was that I could employ my friends for writing assignments. Tom Baake, whom I'd known since high school, worked as a freelance writer, and after I'd worked a couple of months as editor, I arranged a job interview for him with Todd. During the interview, the faithful Tom extolled my virtues to Todd.

"Ah, I don't expect Chris to stay for long," said Todd.

Tom, knowing I was enjoying the work, asked why.

"Well, that Chris... he's the type of guy who never stays in one place too long," Todd answered, his eyebrows flexing. "Yep, he's... he's a rambler."

When Tom later related the story to me, I felt like the hero of a country western ballad. And while I thought the label of a rambler was hilarious, I wondered how Todd Watkins could so misread my nature. I wasn't a rambler! From that point on, I was determined to demonstrate my stalwart nature. I would be the most reliable, conscientious editor he had ever employed.

TIP: If you're renting your house on your own, have prospective applicants fill out an application, insist on a current credit report, and thoroughly check all references. Get an ironclad guarantee that without mutual agreement, the tenancy will end at a certain date. Lastly, consult a trusted real estate professional or a real estate attorney if any of the legalities—and there are many—baffle you.

A month later, I was unceremoniously fired in favor of Todd's son, who had recently been discharged from the navy. Little did I know that I had been there to soften up the territory so he could take over.

As I loaded my belongings into the back of my big station wagon, I couldn't help but laugh at the absurdity of it. Me? A rambler? I was the most stable, reliable guy I knew.

Where Is the Romance Now?

Now, more than 20 years later, I was aboard a jetliner with my family, streaking over the Atlantic, about to move to a new country. Maybe I was a rambler after all, and I had infected my entire family! Cold waves of panic swept over me as I reviewed the arrangements we had made. Insurance? Set. Tenant for the house? Perfect. Work? Stephanie had a job teaching English. I had some freelance assignments set up and my new book to promote. There had to be something else. Oh, yeah. WE DIDN'T HAVE A PLACE TO LIVE!

When your entire life is stowed in the cargo hold of a 747, and your sweet, trusting children are sitting next to you playing Nintendo 64 on the seatback, this missing detail is a concern.

In nearly a year of planning, we had only made one tangential personal contact in Prague: Eva Kacerová. The director of the Masters Degree Program I had completed 12 years earlier had referred her to us, and Eva and I had spoken a few times over the phone. She had kindly offered to let us stay in her apartment for a few days on arrival—though she had never sent the photos she had promised—and said that she had placed some ads in local newspapers on our behalf.

But what if Eva didn't pan out? Was she as sweet and generous as she sounded? Would she meet us at Ruzyne Airport, or was she home laughing about the stupid, gullible Americans?

Before landing in Prague, we first spent a few days in London, but I didn't find the time to see Chris Roberts, Terry's publishing partner, as planned. First off, our biological clocks were still running on California time. Kelsey fell asleep with her face on the table at dinner; Drew, typically even tempered when he's had enough sleep, broke down in tears when he didn't recognize anything on the breakfast menu. Scheduling a trip up to Worcestershire was out of the question.

Besides, we had serious sightseeing to do, and we hit most of the high points: riding double-decker buses, touring the Tower of London, viewing the crown jewels, visiting Madame Tussaud's Wax Museum, and going to the theater, among other things. Stephanie and I had been to Europe before, but the children had never been out of the U.S. Suddenly, everything they encountered was different: the architecture, the food, the cars. Riding in the tube, or taking a taxi, was an adventure, not just a means of transportation. The children were wonderful to be with because we could see everything through their eyes. After all our meticulous planning, our life abroad was now beginning to feel real.

Here we were in London with a different life full of promise and new experience. Somehow, we knew it would all work out— and even if it didn't, it would make an interesting story. "Yeah, remember the time we made those HUGE plans to move to Prague and ended up coming home in a week?"

TIP: As you gear up for departure, post maps, photos, and posters of your destination around the house. Read books, newspapers, and watch movies from your destination country. Listen to the native music.

Expat Answers: What simple advice would you give expatriates when it comes to finding housing? "Get a good agent; don't be rushed. A house is essential to a successful stay for the whole family."
—Michael Paprok, Prague

TIP: For your children, assemble a collection of photos showing friends, relatives, pets, and favorite places back home. They'll get comfort from them and can use them at their new school to introduce themselves to classmates.

A Panelak with a View

But the whole plan seemed to be coming to fruition when Eva, as promised, met us at Prague's Ruzyne Airport with a van and driver. Tall, attractive, and witty, she'd spent years coordinating the Karlovy Vary international film festival, working occasionally as an interpreter for celebrity visitors, and she knew everything there was to know about Prague.

She took us to her apartment on the outskirts of the city—a place she and her husband, Petr, had waited years to get back in communist times—and let us stay there while we got our feet on the ground.

The apartment was in a prefabricated building, the kind of plain, concrete-slab construction I'd only seen in television news about the Soviet Union. The parking lot was completely inadequate for the post-socialist era, and tiny, oddly shaped cars were parked three deep. Residents left them in neutral so they could push them out of the way in order to make space.

Well, we didn't have a car, so that wasn't a problem for us. We unloaded the van and dragged the suitcases into the dark lobby, where we jammed into a small elevator that was lined with scarred red felt. It smelled as though the sweat of a million passengers had soaked into the walls. In the upstairs corridor, Eva's apartment had a massive steel door with several locks on it, and as she worked the keys, my heart sank. I hadn't expected a tree-shaded villa, but I hadn't anticipated a prison cell, either. I imagined a gloomy place with gray walls and a single light bulb dangling from a wire.

Much to our delight, the apartment was simple but cheerful. Kelsey immediately claimed the smaller bedroom and started to make herself at home, arranging some of the stuffed animals she had brought on the bed and putting away her clothes. The small kitchen opened onto a little patio with a view of a park nearby, and Eva pointed out the way to the supermarket, a restaurant, and a McDonald's. After showing us how to operate the shower, the phone, and the locks on the formidable door, and arranging to meet us early the next morning for a day of apartment hunting, Eva returned to her home in Mukarov, a small suburb outside Prague where she lives with her husband. They kept the apartment for the use of their daughter, Tereza, who would soon start university, and for visitors like us.

As she shut the door and we worked the locks behind her, I thought, This is the stupidest thing I've ever done. Here we are in a tiny apartment in a city we've never visited. Where is the romance now? Where is the adrenaline-inducing excitement? Where, for that matter, is Prague, reputed to be one of the most beautiful cities on earth? From the airport, we had passed only through the outskirts, and to us, most of it looked like this apartment—gray and indistinct. What in the world were we doing here?

It was already dark outside, and everyone was hungry. Eva had said there was a small restaurant across the street. We left the apartment, rode down in the smelly elevator, and sidled past the sea of cars to the busy street. Holding the children's hands, we crossed to a small concrete-walled shopping center, forebodingly dark. "I guess it's in there," I said.

Stephanie looked around warily. "We don't know where we are."

"Let's get out of here."

A block or so away, the bright and familiar golden arches of McDonald's beckoned. So much for immersion in the native

TIP: You'll probably leave behind a fistful of keys for everything from cars to bike locks to storage units. Put them all together, label them, and put them in a bank safety deposit box. That way you only need to find a safe place to keep the key to the safety deposit box.

MORE DATA, PLEASE...
Web resources change constantly. For information about movers, freight shippers, and message boards, take a look at www.expatexchange.com. Also, try a Web search using "international relocation" or "overseas moving" to find other sites.

TIP: Instead of appointing a friend to look after your property in your absence, hire a professional manager. You don't want to destroy a friendship over a tenant's clogged drain.

MORE DATA, PLEASE...

For complete information about required vaccinations, health alerts, and other travel-related health concerns, refer to the Centers for Disease Control and Prevention at www.cdc.gov/travel.

culture. We made our way over there as fast as possible. As we waited for our order in the brightly lit restaurant, the children played in the small playground adjacent to the place.

"It's only the first night," I said to Stephanie. "We'll find our way around. We really will."

She was more upbeat about it than I expected. "I know. It's just so strange."

Ano[3], We Have Bananas

Early the following morning, I walked to the nearby supermarket that Eva had pointed out to us. Armed with cash and shopping bags, I was prepared for anything. This was a new day—our first day in our new country. I expected little difficulty in finding my way around the supermarket. Then I encountered the shopping carts. All of them had a locking device on the handle. A chain connected the cart to the next cart in line. When you inserted a coin, the lock unlatched. You got the coin back when you returned the cart. A nifty plan—cuts down on shopping cart theft, I imagine, and saves the employees from having to chase down all the carts in the parking lot. But I didn't have any coins. Eventually, I managed to stop one of the harried shoppers and get change for a note. Having overcome this first obstacle, I proudly pushed the cart ahead of me, ready to hit the aisles.

I expected to find little more than some turnips and a long line at the meat counter—that's pretty much what the out-dated guidebooks we'd read had promised. But to my delight, the place was fully stocked. I wandered up and down the aisles, marveling at how different everything looked and trying to make out the contents based on the pictures

---

[3] "Yes" in Czech.

on the unfamiliar looking labels. I found some cereal—Globs—that, from the picture on the box, contained every bit as much sugar as the stuff the kids were used to back home. I had to buy it for the name alone. I found milk in un-refrigerated cardboard cartons, plus sugar, coffee, and some other stuff. Lastly, I picked up a bunch of bananas.

I was really feeling as though I had conquered this supermarket thing. As the checker rang up the purchases, I positioned myself at the end of the counter, ready to gather everything up and stuff it into the bags. I'd learned to be prepared to bag my own groceries when Stephanie and I had spent a few weeks in France with Drew when he was a baby. Then, a strange thing happened. The clerk seemed to be examining the bananas. I thought she was looking for bruises, but that wasn't it.

She said something to me, then gestured toward the produce department. I had no idea what she was talking about. One of the other customers chattered away at me. I shrugged and said automatically, "No comprendo," my high school Spanish supplanting the rudimentary Czech I had learned in the previous few months.

The clerk put the bananas aside and harrumphed as she pointed to the register total. I paid and left the store, mystified as to what banana-purchasing protocol I had violated. My confidence evaporated, and I felt like a foreigner again.

Later that morning, Eva arrived to take us apartment hunting. She had set up several appointments around the city. "I put in a very good ad," she explained, "saying that you are visiting professors."

If I were a professor, surely I'd know how to buy bananas. I told Eva about my adventure in the supermarket. "Is it not

TIP: If you have a few valuable pieces of art, lend them to a friend for safekeeping in your absence. Make sure they're insured, but there's probably less likelihood of damage in someone's home than in storage.

TIP: If you have young children, arrange for them to be with a baby-sitter on moving day.

banana season or something? Do they only sell them at certain times of the day?" I was perplexed.

But it was nothing so complicated. Customers are just expected to weigh produce items themselves. Every produce department is equipped with an electronic scale. After weighing your item, you hit a little pictogram, and the machine spits out a bar-coded label, Eva explained.

"But I didn't see a scale," I told her.

"Just say, 'Gde je vata?' "

"Right," I said. I'd look for the scale next time, not confident at all that I could remember a sentence that seemed so complex. But if we wanted any fruit or vegetables for the next year, I guessed I'd better remember to use it.

A Potent Mixture of Decay and Beauty

That day, Eva shepherded all of us around Prague, touring the apartments she had arranged for us to see all around the city. We smiled pleasantly at our prospective landlords as Eva would engage them in long conversations and translate the owners' recitation of the apartments' virtues.

The excursion was entirely by public transportation, and along the way she gave us an overview of the city. Most of the day was a blur, as we navigated through what seemed like a bewildering network of trams, metro trains, and buses. Eva took pains to show us on our map where we were, but before long I was totally turned around. This city seemed utterly incomprehensible to me. Prague is divided into 15 districts, with Prague 1 in the center and other districts pieced around it. One moment, we would be in Prague 3, then Prague 6, then Prague 7. After a while, I couldn't tell one from the other. Besides the onslaught of information, the heat was getting to all of us.

Despite these faults, the city was still beautiful, with a grand nineteenth century feel to its architecture. As Stephanie wrote much later in a letter to her uncle, the city had "a potent mixture of decay and beauty." Signs of renewal were everywhere; scaffolding covered the blackened faces of buildings, and many of the streets were dug up as workmen toiled below ground on pipes and wires.

But where were we going to call home?

Before coming to Prague, Stephanie and I had imagined living in the city center in some decrepit Victorian building with bad plumbing and a breathtaking view. Or with breathtaking plumbing and a bad view. But in the center of the city.

```
Subject: Just checking
Date: Mon, 11 Aug 1997 12:06:29
From: Chris Westphal
To: Terry Harris

Dear Terry,
We have surfaced in the Czech Republic. I've already
met the manager of the Globe Bookstore; he's interest-
ed in hosting a reading, etc. Anyway, I'm beat right
now—it was a hassle setting up the e-mail.
-CRW
```

However, we soon learned that capitalism and the influx of foreign employees with fat expense accounts had exacerbated a severe housing shortage. Besides, Kelsey suffers from mild asthma, and when we learned that brown coal was still burned to provide heat in central Prague, living in the center was out of the question.

There was nothing very promising that first day, and we returned to Eva's apartment exhausted and disillusioned. But there were still more apartments to see, and we were set to meet Eva again the following day. Besides finding a place to live, though, there was a lot more to do. Stephanie had to meet with the director of the Caledonian School, the private language institute where she would be teaching English, to make various arrangements and learn what her schedule would be. I was in the midst of a freelance writing project that I planned to complete over the Internet. Most importantly, we had to contact the International School of Prague, scheduled to start in only three weeks. Kelsey and Drew were already enrolled, but we wanted to at least take a look at the place.

Finding the campus turned out to be an aggravating ordeal. We attempted to call the school several times but got no answer. I had found the school via links with the U.S. State Department, with which it is affiliated. Months before leaving the U.S., we had sent in applications, which included letters of recommendation from the children's teachers and principals. Kelsey and Drew were accepted. I had even sent in a check to cover the initial tuition payment. Later, in various e-mails, I had inquired about everything from uniforms (they didn't have them) to meals (there was a cafeteria). All of my written correspondence had gone through the State Department in Washington, DC, and I had never thought to ask about the physical address. The school's Web site noted that ISP was split between two buildings, but the addresses were not listed, probably for security reasons.

Now the school didn't seem to exist anywhere. Eva had never heard of it. No one at the Caledonian had ever heard of it.

The days clicked past. The laundry built up. Tempers flared. At the Caledonian, someone recommended the British School, which happened to be quite near a two-bedroom apartment that we had visited in the Modrany area on the outskirts of Prague.

Enchanted Tourists

The apartment, like most of the others, was located in a complex of panelaks, the slang name for the bleak Soviet-style apartment buildings that dot the Czech landscape the way strip malls do in California. Unlike most we had seen, though, it was nicely renovated with clean white walls, new carpet, and good furniture and appliances.

Rent, including TV, VCR, and linens, was $600. In an economy where a doctor earns $300 per month, it was an outrageous sum, but it was well within our budget. Though it was small—around 750 square feet—it was the nicest apartment we had seen. By then, we had tentatively arranged to send the children to the British School, having all but given up on ISP. We took the apartment.

Within a couple of days, we were moved in, and it felt wonderful to at last unpack our suitcases and settle in. We thought we had cleared the highest hurdle: finding a place to live. We spent a few days exploring the city, thanks to help from Eva and from reading the listings in the English language *Prague Post*.

Daily life seemed to take on an almost magical quality—but that was largely because we weren't really living a normal life. The children hadn't started school. Stephanie hadn't started work. We were still tourists, enchanted by everything we saw.

Riding the clattering trams as they twisted through the narrow streets amid a sea of people and cars was simply breathtaking. We walked through the city in a sort of euphoric daze, unable to believe that we had uprooted our family, rented our house, and traveled halfway around the world to make real this long-cherished fantasy.

Stephanie found a listing for an English language church, and we decided to go in hopes of meeting some new people. That Sunday morning, we made our way into the center of the city and found Saint Michael's Lutheran Church tucked along a narrow, cobbled street. There were several families there, and Drew and Kelsey went off with the children for Sunday School while the regular service continued. Afterward, we introduced ourselves to the congregation. Naturally, the subject of schools came up. The Pastor, Jim Krikava and his wife, Peggy, had two children at ISP. Another family, the Malotts, also had two children attending ISP.

"Well," we wanted to know, "how come they never answer the phone?" We told them about our frustrations in contacting the school.

"Oh, it's an entirely new campus. The phones are new, and they haven't gotten them operating yet," said Steve Malott, who was with the State Department. The blame rested with the state-run Czech phone system, he said, not with the school, which both families and their children said was absolutely wonderful.

The next day, thanks to directions from the Krikavas, we navigated via bus and metro to visit ISP. There, in a pastoral setting just outside Prague's city limits, was a huge, modern campus that rivaled the nicest schools in the U.S. When we toured the campus, we learned that ISP had only moved in the previous February, and this was to be their first full academic year at the new facility. The school has a U.S. public school curriculum, with all classes in English. However, since students from some 60 countries were enrolled, there was a vigorous and very successful English as a second language program.

After seeing the school, the children were enthusiastic about going there. The arrangements had already been made—it was a good thing we hadn't been able to contact them, or we might have cancelled. But the problem was, it was nowhere near our new apartment. Stephanie and I half-heartedly extracted promises from Kelsey and Drew that they wouldn't complain about the long commute time to and from the school, and we decided to send them there.

A few days later—just as all of us had reached our fill of tourist activities and round-the-clock togetherness—classes began at ISP. For a week—partly in penance for having chosen the apartment we did, partly as an economy measure—I took them to school via public transport, which took over an hour. At six o'clock, we were aboard a packed bus to the nearest metro station. After a 15 minute trip, we had to run through the station to catch another line. At the end of that line, we boarded another bus for the rest of the journey. We arrived, exhausted, just as the bell rang. Then I had to do the whole thing in reverse. I'd get back to the apartment and work for a couple of hours before heading out again to fetch the children after classes.

Counting the few minutes it took to walk between the apartment and the bus stop, plus the various waiting times between buses or metro trains, almost five hours of my day was taken up riding public transportation. This was more penance than I was willing to pay. Reluctantly, we contracted through the school for a taxi service, and every morning the cheerful, perpetually half-shaven Milos and his battered Skoda would arrive at 6:45 to drive the children from our apartment in Prague 4 to their school on the edge of Prague 6, an hour or more each way. Still, it was better than running between bus and metro stops.

Despite our out-of-the way location and the apparent suspicion that we aroused among our neighbors, we liked our panelak life. It was so utterly different than the one we had in California that comparisons seemed pointless; inconveniences—whether it was lugging groceries up seven stories when the elevator failed or dealing with surly waiters—were just a part of the charm of being immersed in a new culture. Little did we know that that breezy acceptance of things is also a part of the inevitable culture shock that goes along with living abroad.

```
Subject: Re: Just checking
Date: Wed, 13 Aug 1997 07:36:35
From: Terry Harris
To: Chris Westphal

Hi Chris,
Sorry you missed Charles when you were in the UK. As
it happens I was also there that weekend. Glad you
arrived in CZ ok; hope all is going well.
Terry
```

Getting from Here to There

Loving everything we saw helped us cope with the sensory and emotional overload of our first weeks abroad. We lived in a sort of enchantment that let us look past the graffiti, cope with the crowds on the buses, and tolerate all of the petty inconveniences of adapting to life in a new country. But one thing that it didn't pay to ignore was the reputation of Prague taxi drivers. If ever there was a group legendary for its dishonesty, this was it, and it was better to be wary than victimized. In one instance, a colleague of Stephanie's was charged 5,000 Kc (Czech Crowns—about $150) for a 20-minute taxi ride from the airport to the city center.

Their unsavoriness went beyond simple greed, however. In one widely publicized event, a taxi driver was videotaped bludgeoning a pedestrian with a tire iron for crossing the street too slowly. We didn't want to get fleeced or beaten up, so we resolutely avoided taking taxis, and we definitely hopped to it when we were in the crosswalk. Besides, taxis were for tourists. We were going native as much as possible.

Usually, public transportation was best anyway. If we timed our bus and metro connection right, we could travel from our apartment to the city center within half an hour, riding the clunky Russian-made Metro cars and listening to the singsong recorded voice calling out the stations. We would emerge from the Republiky Station, face the black spires of the tenth century "Powder Tower"—which, as part of the now demolished city walls had contained gun powder—and look down the bustling cobbles of Na Prikope, a street which covers what was once a moat. We had come to live amid this splendid city—to go to concerts in its beautiful halls, to visit castles and museums, cafes and pubs, and simply to be a part of a place that was exciting and different. Within a couple of weeks, I had arranged at the English language Globe Bookstore to do a reading and had met with the editor of the *Prague Post*, who was interested in reviewing *Echo Valley*.

This was what we had come for.

```
Subject: Promotion Copies of EV
Date: Sun, 31 Aug 1997 09:40:30
From: Chris Westphal
To: Terry Harris

Dear Terry &/or Charles,
... I wonder if you could send me a half-dozen copies
that I will use for promotion? 2 remaining.
Regards,
Chris
```

In the Moving Mood

Preparing to move overseas is a little like preparing to bungee jump off, say, the Empire State Building, but you've got to pack more thoughtfully. Moving to another country is not like moving across town. It's more like moving to another planet.

Expect to be overwhelmed periodically by the vastness of it, because unless you're able to treat leaving for a year like going to the beach for the weekend, you'll have to alter virtually everything in your daily life and start over—just like you do when you have children. Even the smallest errands can end up taking an inordinate amount of time. Early on, I had to find some telephone adapters so we could get Internet access. At home, it would have taken a five-minute stroll down the aisle at the local Radio Shack. In Prague, I had to go to three different stores and use various signs, symbols and drawings in order to make myself understood. Magnify this kind of experience times the thousand little things you do every day and you'll get an idea of how overwhelming life abroad can be at the start.

Home Is Where the Equity Is

It's difficult to leave your home for a brief vacation, but to make the arrangements to leave for an entire year is a gargantuan task. There seemed to be no end to the packing, or to the paperwork—everything from making sure the taxes got paid to canceling the utilities and the phone. As we prepared to leave, I wished we could just burn our place down rather than figure out what to do with it, but insurance companies get nasty about that kind of thing. Here are some things to consider if you own your home and plan to live abroad:

Find a house sitter.

So what if they drink the liquor? It's bad for you anyway. The thing about house sitters that has always seemed a little odd is that you give someone free rent and utilities, and then pay them for the privilege. A house sitter isn't a bad idea if money isn't a problem. Consider, also, letting a relative or other person of high moral virtue take care of the place in your absence.

Sell the house!

This is ideal if you're truly intrepid and don't mind cutting all ties to your home. While we were away, though, it was comforting to know that we had a piece of real estate back home—even though our house is on a flood plain and California was in the midst of the wettest winter on record. If you do seriously want to sell your house and start over on your return, keep in mind that your children might not be so sanguine about the idea of having no place to return to.

Rent the house.

Though we weren't terribly fond of our actual house, which had suffered several remodels by design-challenged previous owners, we love our neighborhood. For us, renting out our home was the ideal option. Rent almost covered our mortgage, taxes, insurance, and maintenance, and we got significant tax advantages, too. Unfortunately, most people interested in renting for only a year presented some artful variation of the "just getting back on our feet" story, so finding a good tenant was difficult.

Unable to find a worthy tenant on our own, and with only a few weeks to go before departure, we contacted a reputable real estate agent who, within a few days, found us an outstanding tenant. For a five percent fee, the agent collected the rent, paid house-related bills through a joint checking account that we had opened, and took care of scheduling maintenance, etc., in our absence.

If Less Is More, Think How Much More
More Would Be

To find a mover, we first asked our real estate agent for recommendations, then contacted a nearby military base and asked what mover they used when they sent personnel overseas. Another good starting place would be the human resources or corporate relocation departments of major corporations.

We left for Prague with only what we could carry on the airplane, and in an effort to economize, we shipped nothing. That meant that that unless we were sleeping under bridges, we'd have to find a furnished apartment.

Once established in Prague, we realized how atypical our method was. Diplomatic personnel we met literally shipped stuff over by the ton. One thing we would do differently now is to use an airfreight company and ship less crucial items to be held in storage until we were settled. (See Chapter Thirteen for more information on the art of shipping.)

On the broader scale, here's a basic timeline and checklist for moving and storing your possessions (adapted from the American Moving and Storage Association Moving Planner):

Eight Weeks prior to Moving

- Solicit estimates from several moving companies.
- Contact your insurance agent, and ask him or her about your home-owner's policy to determine whether your possessions are covered by your insurance when moving. If not, make appropriate arrangements to ensure that they are.
- Establish a file for all moving papers and receipts.
- Fill out post office change of address cards.
- Clean out closets and dispose of all items that you will not be taking with you or putting in storage.

Six Weeks prior to Moving

- Hold a moving/garage sale or donate items to charities.

Four Weeks prior to Moving

- If you're moving substantially your entire household overseas, don't pack yourself. If you're putting things in storage and doing the move yourself, get boxes, twine, labels, markers, etc.
- Start packing.

- If your mover is doing the packing, arrange for it to be done one or two days before loading begins.
- Gather valuable personal papers that you may need overseas, including medical and dental records, school records, birth certificates, etc.
- If you're going to store your car, get appropriate documents from your state motor vehicle department.
- Schedule transfer or cancellation of utilities.
- Send change of address cards to friends and relatives, cancel or forward magazine subscriptions.
- Arrange to have a cleaning service come to the house the day after you move out.
- Arrange for your tenant to take houseplants, lend them to friends, or give them away.
- Dispose of all items too dangerous to move, including flammable liquids.

Two Days prior to Moving

- Cancel newspaper delivery.
- Have mover pack your goods (unless you're doing it yourself).
- Defrost and dry refrigerators and freezers to be moved.
- Set aside valuable items to carry with you, including jewelry, vital documents, money, and valuable small items.

Moving Day

- Be on hand to answer questions, give directions to movers, and stay until they are finished.
- Complete information on bill of lading and carefully read the document before you sign it.
- Make sure you have your copies of the bill of lading and inventory.
- Keep the bill of lading until your possessions are delivered, the charges are paid, and any claims are settled.
- Before the van leaves, take one final look through the house to make certain nothing has been left behind.
- Have cleaning service clean the house.
- Go through with your tenant and check each room for damage. List damage on a list that both you and your tenant sign.
- Make arrangements to stay away from home for a day or so after you've moved out of your house.

Delivery Day

- Be on hand to answer any questions and hope the movers speak your language, or have someone to help with translation.
- Supervise unloading and unpacking.
- Check carefully for any damaged or missing items.
- Note on the inventory any damaged boxes or obvious damage to unboxed items before you sign anything.

Looking around our empty house, we couldn't believe that we had actually done it. Maybe we had imagined this day, but never in this stark detail. The van was hardly out of the driveway before the tenant arrived and immediately began making himself at home.

Some friends were on vacation and were kind enough to let us stay in their home for the few days immediately preceding our departure. There, feeling as though we were in exile, we tied up last minute loose ends. Our last act before moving was putting a huge box full of linens and other things we would need on our return in the front of the storage barn in the back yard of our home. We knew that when we returned, it might take a couple of days for us to receive our furnishing and other belongings from storage.

But that day seemed very, very far away.

THREE

Hobnobbing with the Foreign Police

"You know you're an expat when... you can't remember whether the month or the day comes first when you write the date in numbers."
—Kage Glantz, Denmark

The Czech Republic's foreign police, who regulate immigration and police matters related to foreigners, are housed in a huge, nondescript building near Hlavni Nadrazi, the main train station in Prague. The foreign police headquarters is little more than a giant box assembled of the ubiquitous prefabricated concrete panels that define Czech communist-era architecture.

Some factory somewhere once churned out millions of these square panels in various sizes. Architects were left the dismal job of figuring out unique ways to fit them together. In this case, they put together four identical boxes labeled A, B, C, and D inside the main building. Kafka meets Dr. Seuss.

We needed no visa to enter the Czech Republic, but if we wanted to stay for longer than three months or work in the country, we had to get permanent resident status.

```
Subject: Reading at the Globe
Date: Sat, 06 Sep 1997 19:44:20
From: Chris Westphal
To: Terry Harris

Dear Terry,
Just returned from The Globe, the English language
bookstore here in Prague where I met the manager...
and we've set up a reading for October 9. Is this a
practical date? I think that should allow you to get
an adequate number of books to the store... I'd say
20... 25? I'm sure he'll contact you by e-mail, too.
Hope all's well.
Regards,
CRW
```

Stephanie was eligible for permanent resident status, and the children and I would be able to apply, too. The Caledonian, Stephanie's Prague school, helped her with the paperwork, but that was only part of the story. It had taken us the better part of our first month in Prague, prowling the labyrinthine streets of the city, searching for offices that always seemed to be hidden in courtyards or behind scaffolding, to acquire the proper documents, stamps, and translations we needed to legally live here. We needed:

- a residency application, written in Czech. Marie Novak, our landlady, had helped us fill these out.
- a notarized lease, showing we had a place to live and wouldn't be camping out in the metro stations.
- documentation of financial assets totaling a year's minimum Czech salary—calculated at $1,000.
- a document proving that I wasn't a criminal—at least, not a criminal in the Czech Republic.
- a translated and certified copy of our marriage certificate.
- translated and certified copies of the children's birth certificates.
- multiple passport-sized photos, and probably a few other things I've forgotten about.

```
Subject: Globe has books
Date: Sat, 27 Sep 1997 08:18:36
From: Chris Westphal
To: Terry Harris

... Echo Valley is displayed in the window of The
Globe next to James Joyce, Umberto Eco and Wm
Faulkner. Good company.
-CRW
```

Now, as we maneuvered our way through the corridors of Building B, Stephanie and I felt a keen sense of accomplishment. Anyone can get a simple visa for three months. All you have to do is show up and get a stamp in your passport. That was tourist stuff. It takes some determination to stay longer. With our gathered documents secure in several plastic sleeves, we waited in line in front of Office 8.

As each triumphant applicant emerged, new-won residency permits in hand, we shared their victory. Yes, we thought, soon, we also will each possess a cool green *prukaz*, or residency permit, which resembles a passport. People who flash a prukaz also get substantial discounts at tax-supported events, such as the opera and symphony.

Our turn was next. We could almost feel the embossed paper and smell the fresh ink of the inevitable stamps that would endorse the document. Another triumphant couple emerged. We eagerly started walking forward to the door. Then, from out of nowhere, a Czech woman barged ahead of us, waving a sheaf of papers. Stephanie and I were incensed, but couldn't say anything.

Fuming, we stood there and waited. Finally, the interloper emerged. We scowled at her and entered the office. An attractive young woman—slender, blonde, about 22 or so—sat behind the desk. Fortunately, she spoke English well and didn't seem to resent that we hadn't learned Czech. She asked for the various documents, which we dutifully retrieved and set before her.

As she sorted through the papers, there was a momentary lull. I looked up at her bulletin board, where she had posted a picture of a castle. Always on the lookout for stuff to do with the kids, I asked where it was. Just a half hour out of Prague, she said. It was Karlstein Castle, one of the residences of Charles IV in the fourteenth century, but mainly a "safe" to protect the royal insignia during war and other times of danger. "We should take the children there," I said to Stephanie.

She looked at one of the pictures of the kids. "Ah, I've seen you on the bus with your children," she said. "I live near you."

ACCORDING TO THE EXPERTS... TV SYSTEMS ARE DIFFERENT IN DIFFERENT PARTS OF THE WORLD. THE U.S. USES THE NTSC SYSTEM, WHILE MOST OF EUROPE USES PAL. FRANCE, AS USUAL, GOES ITS OWN WAY WITH SOMETHING CALLED SECAM. ALL THOSE ACRONYMS BOIL DOWN TO THIS: YOUR U.S. TV AND VCR WON'T WORK IN EUROPE. FOR ADAPTERS, PLUS TVS AND OTHER APPLIANCES THAT WILL WORK WORLDWIDE, TAKE A LOOK AT WWW.APPLIANCESOVERSEAS.COM/CATALOG99.HTML.

MORE DATA, PLEASE... Pimsleur language instructional tapes in 27 languages, as well as other materials for learning foreign languages, are available at www.languagetapes.com/index.html.

Stephanie Asks a Surprising Question

Stephanie expressed her surprise that we were so conspicuous; so much for blending in with the natives. We asked the clerk's name and she told us it was Edith. Stephanie smiled. "I'm Stephanie." Edith gestured to the forms on her desk. She knew our names. In fact, she knew everything about us. If this were 10 years earlier, she'd probably know our bathing habits.

Then Stephanie asked something astonishing, "Do you babysit?"

My jaw dropped to the floor. Okay, it wasn't a Stalinist state anymore, but that didn't necessarily mean that the foreign police had turned into sweet Officer O'Casey, helping the school children cross the street and scratching the cocker spaniel. Did we want an operative of the state cooking up macaroni and cheese for our kids and asking questions about our political beliefs? And I thought I was the impulsive one!

If Edith was surprised by this invitation, she didn't show it. She seemed flattered to have been asked about her childcare experience. Why, yes, she said, she did babysit from time to time. "I worked for a year as a nanny in England," she said. "That's where I learned English."

Now, if ever there was a perfect cover to get into the homes of foreigners, this was it. Edith jotted down her phone number and handed it to us. Stephanie was about to give her our number, and Edith again indicated the documents. "I have yours." She smiled good-naturedly.

Sitting there, I tried to make sense of Stephanie's strategy. In asking Edith to babysit, was she trying to ease us through the bureaucracy? Was she just chatting? Or was I being paranoid about this country's past and the role of the police in enforcing it?

Would Edith make sure our papers got processed quickly now that we had virtually invited her over? As I delved into dark possibilities of having Edith babysit, she examined our statement from the stockbroker, which was fat with the recent run-up in prices.

Puzzled, she pointed to the form. I expected her to say something like, "You have enough here for a small village. What kind of capitalist pig are you?" Instead she said, "I don't see the balance. Could you show me, please?"

I pointed to the line. She nodded. Then, with a smile, she reached for the assorted stamps on her desk. Systematically, she stamped various documents and swiftly filed them away. Everything was approved. We were now legal residents of the Czech Republic. We weren't tourists anymore. Despite the effort that had gone into reaching this milestone, we didn't quite feel as though we deserved it yet. We struggled with the language. We were still just learning our way around the city. Did we really deserve this distinction? Edith seemed to think so. Handing us our documents, she smiled politely and said we could pick up the residency permits a month from then in Office 10. Another chance to visit this place was good news indeed.

"Great," I said.

"And nice to meet you," Stephanie said.

As we got out onto the street, I told Stephanie, "That may not have been the smartest thing in the world, asking if the Foreign Police want to come to our house to look after our children. Police here have something of a reputation," I reminded her.

"Yeah. Maybe I won't call her."

"I think that's best," I said.

TIP: Driving across the Czech Republic, I was stopped by the police. Though I had done nothing, the officer demanded a 1000 crown payment—about $30—or I would be arrested. Americans call this bribery. If faced with this situation, do as I did: pay the money, and consider it a users' tax or a fee to protect your rights.

MORE DATA, PLEASE...

For international phone and electrical information and supplies, take a look at www.voltagevalet.com/idx.html. Voltage Valet Division, Hybrinetics, Inc., 225 Sutton Place, Santa Rosa, CA 95407, Tel: (Toll-free in the U.S.) 800.247.6900, Tel: (International) +707.585.0333, Fax: 707.585.7313

The Right Start

The night before we left for Prague, I was busy tearing the packaging from over-the-counter medications we would bring, trying to save space. I hadn't done this since taking a 50-mile hike with the Boy Scouts.

There are plenty of excellent over-the-counter medications outside the United States. Unfortunately, if you don't know the language, it's difficult to know how to ask for them, so bring at least a starter supply with you.

If we had to make a list of priorities in terms of luggage, Stephanie would probably put a computer and shoes at the top, and not necessarily in that order. We wanted to pack the most computer power possible in our limited space, and managed to squeeze into our luggage two laptop computers, a travel printer, and a scanner, plus all the necessary cables, papers, and ink cartridges.

Most of the equipment needed only simple plug adapters, but the scanner required a "constant use" voltage adapter—a clunky black transformer that looked like it belonged in a Frankenstein movie. Other electrical appliances were either furnished with our apartment or we purchased them there. In Prague, we bought an iron—no home is complete without one in Europe—a coffeemaker, a small portable stereo, an alarm clock, a phone, and a telephone answering machine.

We probably could have shipped all of these items from home, but would have had to not only pay shipping, but also find various adapters, which can be expensive.

Expat Answers: *What are some of the most important things to bring from home?*

- *one real memento of your home city, preferably a good picture*
- *medical records*
- *address book*
- *comfortable shoes*
- *small favorite food items*
- *your sense of humor*

–Various respondents

You Say Potato, I Say Brambory

Our new landlady, Marie Novak, taught English at Charles University in Prague—the oldest university in Europe—and promptly started Stephanie and me on lessons in Czech. Using an excellent series of language tapes from the Pimsleur Company, we had learned some of the basics and were naively confident that within a few months we'd be chatting away in Prague's many pubs and cafes.

Unfortunately, once we opened our mouths, the game was up. People would either answer us in English, being eager to practice the language, or be completely baffled by whatever we were saying; we thought it was Czech, but apparently it was gibberish. If we'd been in Paris, maybe people would have been rude to us, but here that wasn't the case. Still, the inability to make yourself understood is enormously frustrating.

One time, Stephanie was in a store and wanted to buy some chicken. No matter how she tried to phrase the request, all she got was blank stares. Finally, she tucked her hands under her arms, flapped her elbows, and clucked. We had chicken for dinner that night.

I took language classes for several months—first with Marie, then at the Caledonian—before coming to the conclusion that I was past my prime for language acquisition and finally throwing in the towel. I really felt like a failure in that regard. I had hoped to attain some level of fluency and to return home at least conversational in the language. Instead, I reconciled myself to speaking a sort of pidgin Czech, mangling the sentence structure, mismatching the cases, verbs, and nouns, and generally making a hash of it all.

Stephanie and I were not alone in our neglect of the language. We met many expatriates both at the Caledonian and at ISP who had been in the country for several years and had learned only the bare rudiments of the language.

Should you learn the language of your adopted country? According to expatriates contacted for this book, the answer is "Yes!" Learning the language of your adopted country will ultimately pay big dividends, giving you an opportunity to make friends as well as a significantly greater sense of belonging within the culture.

FOUR

Who Put the Klutz in Kludsky?

"You know you're an expat when... you give up comparing the foreign country with your home country."

–Pam Petrillo, Japan

The Kludsky Family Circus is something of an institution in the Czech Republic and is one of the oldest family circuses in Europe. While riding the bus from our panelak, we had seen the posters and—the funky name notwithstanding—thought it would make great entertainment for the kids. We had been in Prague for about three months and had had our fill of tourist diversions. We were ready to participate in something really authentic.

We took the tram to the park alongside the Vltava River and in the distance could see the big top. As we walked across the parking lot, we heard the roar of an engine. A battered Audi sped across the lot, then suddenly hit a ramp with the passenger-side wheels.

```
Subject: Promotion Copies?
Date: Thu, 02 Oct 1997 07:15:07
From: Chris Westphal
To: Terry Harris

Dear Terry & Charles,
Still have not received 6 promotion copies as men-
tioned earlier. Globe DID receive some books. I meet
the Czech agent today and will have zero books remain-
ing. Also, please forward remainder of advance...
```

We couldn't tell whether this was some kind of pre-circus show or a stunt-driver's practice session. We stood there, amazed not at the stunt itself, but at the complete lack of safety precautions. At home, you get a ticket for not wearing a seatbelt. The driver was wearing a helmet, maybe a seatbelt, but the spectators were on their own; there were no ropes or partitions to protect them. And this driver was no expert. Sometimes the car would slam to the ground right off the ramp. Other times it would veer crazily toward the onlookers.

"Let's get out of here," said Stephanie.

We continued toward the red-and-white striped big top. Over the flaps of the circus tent, big sequined letters spelled out "KLUDSKY." Stephanie and I joked that Kludsky was probably the origin of the word klutz.

"I wonder who the original klutz really was," Stephanie joked.

As we approached the entry to the tent, a clown caught sight of Drew and came toward him. Drew—caught off-guard—dodged the other way. The crowd watched and laughed as the clown, despite those ungainly shoes, scrambled agilely after Drew and finally managed to catch him. Drew tried to squirm free—he didn't seem to really be getting the joke here—but the clown held him in a headlock and put a dab of red lipstick on the tip of his nose. Released, Drew smiled. He was like a wild animal who'd been tagged.

```
Subject: Misc. items
Date: Wed, 08 Oct 1997 10:45:09
From: Chris Westphal
To: Terry Harris

Hi, Terry,
I think a couple of my questions got lost in the shuf-
fle. Or maybe you've been out on business. Anyway,
here goes:
1) Didn't receive any books. I don't mind paying for
them if you could ask Charles to send along 10 to me.
2) If you wish, deduct the amount owing for them from
my advance pmt. due.
3) Are you going to the Frankfurt Book Fair?
```

Once inside the big top, Kelsey spotted her friend from school, Milena Parprok, and we said it would be all right for her to sit with Milena and her parents. Stephanie, Drew, and I found seats—orange, plastic chairs—within inches of the single large ring. Overhead was the trapeze platform—and I mean, directly overhead.

Soon after we found our seats, the announcer, a woman with flaming red hair and a green-sequined gown, emerged from behind the flap of the tent. She was all smiles and dramatic gestures as she prepped the audience for the dazzling show they were about to witness. We couldn't understand anything she said, but at least twice she mentioned the words "Las Vegas!" which either meant that the Circus Kludsky had been there, or would like to go, or had at least heard of the place.

Then she introduced the various acts. I think. Periodically—as though all of us had forgotten that we were at a circus—she would remind us that this was "Circus Kludsky," drawing out the pronunciation of the word Kludsky so it was Kl-l-l—l-u-u-u-u-d-s-SKY!

The acts were absolutely great. First came the trained camels and llamas. We were close enough to smell them as they paraded around the ring, grouping themselves together to the direction of the whip-cracking ringmaster.

Next, a woman did a snake-dancing act, twirling a huge boa constrictor around, giving the impression that, given adequate provocation or a loosened grip, the snake would torpedo right into the audience at any moment.

Then there were juggling dogs, along with bears and horses performing various tricks. All of the acts were first rate, and as we watched them, we concluded that there wasn't a klutz in the bunch.

MORE DATA, PLEASE... For more information about U.S. Overseas Schools, including links about teaching and links to U.S. Overseas Schools by region, log on to the U.S. State Department's site at www.state.gov/www/about_state/schools. Office of Overseas Schools, Department of State, Washington, DC 20522-0132, Tel: 202.261.8200, Fax: 202.261.8224, E-mail: OverseasSchools@state.gov

Expat Answers:
What are the advantages and disadvantages of sending your children to public school in your host country?

"Advantages: You immerse them in the everyday life of typical citizens of that country. You avoid elitist prejudices, religious dogma, and general snobbiness. Disadvantages: Classes may be too large, not enough individual attention, 'American' schools tend to try to out-American the Americans."
–David Howard, Spain

Getting into the Act

Between the various acts, as the uniformed helpers swept the plastic tarp in the ring or pulled it back for the animal acts, were the clowns—three of them, usually. And at one point came audience participation time. Two little girls were selected from the audience, and the clowns demonstrated hula-hoops. The girls—about six and eight—got it on the second try. Then the head clown said something in Czech. Everyone laughed as he looked searchingly around the audience. He headed for the edge of the ring, and a man in the audience suddenly stood, then ran for the door, literally climbing over the chairs as he beat a hasty exit. I became mildly worried. What had the clown said to scare away a paying customer?

The clown made an exaggerated gesture of defeat. Then he turned and started heading for me. I realized he had said something like, "And now I'm going to pluck an adult from the audience and make a fool of him!" I tried to shrink in my chair, but he advanced—the grim reaper in white face and funny shoes. All eyes were on me as the clown gestured dramatically for me to come into the ring.

Not understanding the language wasn't going to get me out of this. Drew was enjoying his dad's embarrassment and pushed me out of my chair. Stephanie had a big grin on her face too. I had nowhere to hide. Stepping over the rail, I slowly moved to the center of the ring. I haven't tried to spin a hula-hoop since I was nine, and I distinctly recall it falling around my ankles after about two gyrations.

But maybe this would be different. The clown handed me an aluminum hula-hoop. This wasn't your cheesy dime store hula-hoop, but a finely balanced performance device, engineered for professional use, test-ed exhaustively by lab-coated clowns under the most trying conditions, and guaranteed to defy gravity.

To the whoops of the crowd, my instructor demonstrated the proper hip-thrusting movement, then invited me to try. I tried once. Twist. Thrust. The thing fell to my ankles. He demonstrated again, instructing me loudly and carefully in Czech. Of course, I understood nothing, but smiled gamely. "Okay," I said. I tried again. I failed again.

Standing there, a fool, I couldn't help but feel how absurdly wonderful this was. Stephanie and Drew were red with laughter; Kelsey and her friend were hunched over together, howling. I had failed totally, and I had done it in front of several hundred people. And I felt this weird bond of silliness with them. It didn't matter that we didn't speak the same language. It didn't matter that back in the U.S., where it was nine hours earlier, our friends were driving to work or taking their children to school. It didn't matter because I was here, under a spotlight with an aluminum hula hoop around my feet. If life is ever about living in the moment, this was a moment to be savored in all its garish absurdity.

But now that I had failed twice, the entertainment value of my performance was diminishing. I figured that was the end of it. But the clown wasn't done with me yet.

He stood on a chair, squatted down holding the back of the chair, and lifted his rear up and down. His clown helper put the hula-hoop around his waist, and he spun it that way.

Then he dismounted and indicated the chair. "You do that," he said to me in English. Maybe it was my dumb-foundedness that convinced him I spoke English.

So, with great fanfare and to the roaring laughter from the crowd, I climbed up on

---

MORE DATA, PLEASE...
A good starting place to learn more about distance learning is the Web site for the United States Distance Learning Association, at www.usdla.org. Founded in 1987, the USDLA has links to dozens of sites with information about all aspects of distance learning, from pre-kindergarten to post-graduate.

The University of Phoenix is the nation's largest "on-line" university, offering undergraduate, certificate, and graduate degrees in a wide variety of disciplines. You don't have to go to Phoenix, either. On-line at www.phoenix.edu/index_flat.html. The University of Phoenix, Tel: (Toll-free in the U.S.) 800.773.2918

The University of Texas "Telecampus" offers on-line courses and programs K-12 and through post-graduate. Log on to their site at www.telecampus.utsystem.edu. The University of Texas TeleCampus, Tel: (Toll-free in the U.S.) 888.839.2716, E-mail: telecampus@utsystem.edu

MORE DATA, PLEASE...
Log on to Johns Hopkins Center for Talented Youth at www.jhu.edu/gifted. Johns Hopkins University Center for Talented Youth, 3400 N. Charles Street, Baltimore, MD 21218, Tel: 410.516.0081, Fax: 410.516.0200

MORE DATA PLEASE...
To get started on your home-schooling research, check out www.homeschool.com, which features links, questions-and-answers, and resources for home-schoolers.

the chair and held onto the back. And as I swiveled and shook, the hoop made a few limp rotations around my derriere. I knew then who the Klutz in Kludsky was. It was I.

Schools of Thought, Thoughts of Schools

Travel is broadening in its own right, but unless you're devoted to home-schooling, you'll probably want your school-aged children in some sort of school program. Various options for educating your children are available while you live abroad.

Prior to departure, we had arranged to send the children to the International School of Prague, ISP, which we had found via the Internet. The school was established by the U.S. Embassy and, like most U.S. Overseas Schools, is now privately operated. I had communicated with the school almost entirely by e-mail.

We briefly considered Czech schools when we arrived, but our landlady persuaded us that the style of instruction was something of a relic of the communist era, so we quickly abandoned that idea. Anyway, when the children finally saw ISP's new $15 million campus, they couldn't wait to start classes.

The U.S. Office of Overseas Schools, a branch of the State Department, assists 180 schools in 130 countries. The schools offer a U.S. curriculum and English language instruction. About half of the teachers are U.S. citizens, and the remainder is from the country where the school is located. Americans are sometimes a minority in terms of student body population. At ISP, there were students from some 60 different countries. As a result, our children got a crash course in cultural diversity second to none.

While we were abroad, California was grappling with bi-lingual education, and voters were asked to decide whether non-English speaking students should receive instruction in their native language. If California had followed

ISP's example, though, there would be no controversy. With students from so many different countries, it would have been impossible to teach in the students' native languages and in English. Instead, ISP immersed all students in the regular classroom. For an hour a day, non-English speaking students received intensive English instruction. The result? Within six months, virtually all of the non-English speaking students were strong conversational speakers. Within two years, they were totally fluent.

American schools range from the American Embassy School in Reykjavik, Iceland, with 10 students, to large overseas schools, such as the Singapore American School, with 2,602 students. It's an excellent system, though it's expensive. Tuition for our children totaled $12,500 each per year. As "freelance" expatriates, we had the rare opportunity to pay this sum ourselves. Almost all of the other parents had the tuition paid either by the U.S. Government, if they were diplomatic personnel, or by their corporation.

Children learn many important things outside of school while living abroad:

- Speaking English louder doesn't make people understand you any better.
- Even if you don't understand the rules, you still have to obey them.
- The most important words in any language are "please" and "thank you."
- People are proud of their country, their culture, and their identity.
- It doesn't feel good to be stereotyped.
- It doesn't matter how they do it at home.
- Your family is the most important thing in the world.

Home Room at Home

The Talking Heads were one of the great bands of the 1980s, and in Same as it Ever Was, a moody song about the currents of life flowing beneath everything, David Byrne sings plaintively, "My God, what have I done?"

We sometimes said the same thing while living abroad. We said it about the first apartment, about not owning a car, and I definitely said it when I lost a pile of Deutchmarks in Hungary to some guy playing a shell game. But we never regretted our choice to send the children to the International School of Prague.

I hope you're so fortunate, but you may not be. There may not be an American school nearby, and the public schools may not be a good fit for your child. Home-schooling is a viable option, and though it would definitely present its challenges, it is a way to ensure that your child doesn't fall behind academically.

Home-schooling has entered the mainstream with sometimes-remarkable results. Home-schooling is accepted in all 50 states and can be approached either with a standardized curriculum or without one. On-line, you can check with advisors, take virtual "field trips," exchange e-mails with other home-schoolers, and of course, have on-line courses.

If you are interested in home-schooling, first check with your local school district for guidelines and resources. They may offer a program free-of-charge. Since mail can be unreliable overseas, it's best to bring along whatever course materials you can.

High Achievers On-line

Both of our children are in Gifted and Talented Education classes in the United States, but there was no GATE program at the International School of Prague. The curriculum was generally excellent, and what little the children might have missed in terms of raw academics was more than compensated for by the experience of living abroad and the various excursions we made to other countries.

If you have an exceptionally gifted child, you may consider enrolling him or her in a structured on-line program to supplement learning. One of the best is offered through the Center for Talented Youth at Johns Hopkins University. CTY accepts only the top two to three percent of students based on their achievement in standardized admissions tests. If your child qualifies, he or she can enroll in advanced on-line writing tutorials in math, grades K through 12, and writing in grades 6 through 12. CTY, through various university campuses such as Stanford University and Loyola-Marymount, also offers intensive summer courses in a number of disciplines, from science and engineering to drama.

This Isn't Your Child's Distance Learning

Surprisingly, according to a recent *60-Minutes* program, only 16 percent of today's college students are the 18 to 22-year-old, dormitory-living, keg party-attending variety. These days, the majority of students in higher education courses are working adults.

Distance, or on-line, education has also grown up, and a number of institutions offer college and post-graduate coursework on-line. For non-working spouses, the isolation of living abroad can be very intense, so the ability to earn an undergraduate or graduate degree while abroad has a lot of innate appeal. If you have children, on-line coursework will give you the flexibility you need to spend time with your family and to find diversions outside the home. Even if you embark upon a distance learning program, don't neglect making outside social contacts. Sitting in front of a computer to the exclusion of all else is no way to experience life at home, and certainly not while living abroad. Now, if they could figure out a way to have a kegger on-line, we'd have the best of both worlds.

FIVE

Use the Good China

"You know you're an expat when... you find yourself talking English very slowly even to your partner."

—Peter Croft, Abu Dhabi

As winter blew its foggy breath our way in November, we were ready to batten down the hatches. This was home, and we were determined to make it work. Living so far away from ISP required precision timing for all concerned. Everyone was out of bed at 6:00 and dressed by 6:15. We had a quick breakfast of Kukrinski Lupinki (corn flakes) or Globs (pellet-shaped things), then dashed down the stairs to meet Milos, the taxi driver who took the children to school, at quarter to seven. Stephanie and I held our breath as the flimsy Skoda vanished into the fog for the hour-long drive around the outskirts of the city to ISP.

Stephanie would usually head out soon thereafter, lugging her big black satchel full of books, with more books in a backpack. She taught some classes at Caledonian's downtown campus, but most of her students were adults. Stephanie would meet them in their offices or in a café, where they practiced English conversation with her.

I usually stayed home, where I had various freelance writing projects underway. In August, I had gotten an English language phone directory, published by the *Prague Post,* which listed various businesses that served the expatriate community. Sending faxes via my computer, I had canvassed all the public relations and advertising agencies and gotten some freelance assignments from a company called Eklektik

Communications. What I really wanted, though, was an office—a place to go and be around other people for at least part of the day.

Instead, I spent my days hunched over the computer, editing the English versions of publications such as the *Slovak Weekly Health Review* and *Czech Telecom Week*. I could hear the Slavic intonations in sentences such as this one from *Czech Telecom Week:* "The principle of calls prepayment will be the same like in phone cards for call-boxes." It was mind-numbing work. In the midst of it, I would look up and gaze through the laundry at Hotel Dum and sometimes wonder just what in the hell we had gone to all this trouble for. I envied the set schedule and the interaction that Stephanie had with others.

About a dozen times a day I'd check my e-mail, hoping for word from Terry Harris, but in the middle of October, he vanished. I kept sending him messages, like sonar pings into a dead ocean. He had made such a great pitch, promised such a vigorous marketing campaign, and asked me to restrain my own efforts because he had a plan.

```
Subject: (no subject)
Date: Fri, 07 Nov 1997 15:15:14
From: Chris Westphal
To: Terry Harris

Hi, Terry,
Still have not received books or last installment of
advance. Of course, neither of these things is life-
and-death, however I do feel I should follow up.
Discouragingly, I haven't received any packages sent
to me from anywhere! Meanwhile, I await the transla-
tion of sample chapters after much delay, at which
point I'll pursue a Czech sale. I signed all 5 books
remaining at Globe to hasten their sale.
If you have any comments or materials from publishers
that would help my sale here (or provide some encour-
agement at least), please let me know and I'll arrange
to receive a fax.
```

I was still making headway promoting my book, however. I had done a well-received reading of *Echo Valley* at the Globe and sold a few books. Through Eva, I'd also found a translator, Vera Chase, who was busy translating two chapters of the book into Czech. Vera had in turn introduced me to a Prague-based literary agent, Kristen Olsen, an American who had lived in Prague for several years. Kristen liked the book and was eager to market it to Czech publishers once the translation was finished. Despite Terry Harris' vanishing act, I still had high hopes of selling *Echo Valley* to one or more European publishers.

Typically, I'd still be at the computer when Stephanie returned in the late afternoon, exhausted after a day of teaching and lugging her books from place to place. The children would stagger through the door around five, throw their books on the couch, and collapse like hardened commuters. I half expected them to ask for a Manhattan.

```
Subject: Anybody home?
Date: Mon, 17 Nov 1997 08:52:28
From: Chris Westphal
To: Terry Harris

Dear Terry,
I've been corresponding with Cynthia and Gordon⁴, and
I'm wondering what is going on. I have gotten no
response to several previous messages. Have they heard
anything? Let me know if there's anything I can do.
```

I was going a little stir-crazy. When everyone else was exhausted, I would want to go out. One day, we were desperate to watch a video. I gamely volunteered to go to Video To Go, an English language video rental store we'd learned about. The round-trip took three hours. We did get to see Burt Lancaster in "The Crimson Pirate," though, so I'd have to say that it was worth the trip.

The greatest problem with living so far out was that every time we wanted to do anything with the children at ISP, it took hours of time. For Halloween, all the parents had arrayed their cars in the parking lot, and the children trick-or-treated trunk to trunk. We didn't have a car, so we were off the hook for that. But we'd missed our bus connection and didn't arrive until most of the candy was already gone. Missing Halloween was a heartbreaker. And the kids were upset about it, too. Stephanie and I felt doubly guilty because in all our time in Prague, the children hadn't been able to have any children over to our house. Kelsey had only gone to Milena's once or twice. It was impossible to deny that we simply lived too far away from the school.

---

⁴Cynthia Kear and Gordon Skene, two other writers whose books Terry Harris had contracted to publish.

```
Subject: Echo Valley: Collector's Item?
Date: Tue, 18 Nov 1997 10:10:35
From: Chris Westphal
To: David Shapiro
```

Dave,
Thought I should pass along to you this insider's tip
that the first edition of *Echo Valley*, published with
much fanfare just four months ago, appears to be headed for collector's item status, owing to the disappearance of the publisher.
It has amassed sales in the dozens (perhaps the scores
or hundreds; who knows, as the publisher is GONE) and
is universally adored by those who have read it, but
it appears that the publisher's reach exceeded his
grasp by some 7,000 miles—and, to judge by his non-
payment of the last bit of my meager advance—by at
least a few hundred dollars, too.
I am severely BUMMED by this turn of events, which has
been unfolding over the past few weeks, as he has
become increasingly non-responsive to my queries.
I e-mailed the two other writers whose books he bought
(and published), and learned that they have had much
the same experience. That is to say, he's not just
giving me the cold shoulder because I'm out here in
the hinterlands. Consensus among his "stable of writers" is that the guy, though not a crook, is perhaps a
manic depressive (???!!!)

Stephanie wasn't happy about having to lug books from one end of the city to the other. The children weren't happy about the long taxi ride and never having friends over. I wasn't happy about being stuck inside all day. We hadn't yet forsaken the proletarian lifestyle, but we were sure starting to think like the bourgeoisie. We were longing for an apartment closer in, and maybe a car, but the economics still seemed to prohibit it.

To recharge our batteries, we rented a puny Opel sedan and battled the wind vortexes of BMWs and Mercedes Benzes on the Austrian autobahn for a three-day weekend in Salzburg. While engaging in the usual touristy things—visiting castles, a salt mine, and lively restaurants—we were struck by how clean the streets and the buildings were. Prague, though spectacular, was still recovering from 40 years of neglect under communist rule. The people and the government—and the dogs, it seemed—were learning to cope with the onslaught of tourists and the introduction of consumer culture. In a word, the city was dirty.

Crossing the Czech border from Austria after a busy and fun weekend, our moods almost immediately plummeted. Off to the side, merchants in flimsy sheds hawked cheap marionettes and lawn gnomes. "It's like driving into Mexico from the U.S.," Stephanie observed quietly.

We hoped that visiting Austria would help us renew our enthusiasm for the Czech Republic. Instead, our zest for the culture seemed to have fermented into something bordering on disdain. We had reached that phase of culture shock when the novelty of our adventure had worn off. Cultural differences no longer enchanted us; they annoyed us. Why WERE the taxi drivers such crooks? Why didn't anyone seem to mind the trash that lined the highways? Why did you have to go all the way to the post office and stand in line to pay the phone bill?

As we continued toward Prague, we saw a prostitute wearing leopard hotpants standing on the shoulder of the road waiting for customers. "What's that lady doing way out here?" asked Kelsey.

"Probably waiting for a bus," I said, trying to sound blasé about it.

"She must be cold, dressed like that."

"I imagine so," I said.

"Can I get some shorts like that?"

"NO."

A few hours later, we entered the tangle of highways funneling into Prague. Miraculously, we found our apartment—using the towering Hotel Dum (pronounced Doom) as a landmark. We were happy to get back home, but when Stephanie and I were alone, we couldn't help but ask each other, "Why are we here?"

The dream was losing its luster. Yes, we were in a foreign country. Yes, there were cool buildings all over the place. But appreciators of cool architecture though we are, we didn't come to be with buildings. We came, when all was said and done, to be with people

We truly had expected it to be different. In our fantasies—well, my fantasies, at least—I had pictured us allied with a coterie of writers and artists—sophisticated and rebellious folks who, like us, had come here to drink in this culture as it underwent a renaissance. Barring that, we would have at least liked to know a few couples and go out to dinner with them and talk about the kids, about travel, about anything. But other than the Krikavas and the Malotts, whom we'd met within two weeks of arriving in Prague, we knew virtually no other expatriates.

In a word, we were lonely. My emotional disarray was exacerbated by the apparent disappearance of Terry Harris. For weeks, despite repeated phone calls, e-mails, and attempted faxes, I had been unable to find out where he was. In some senses, he and *Echo Valley* had become my *raison d'etre* in the country. While I continued freelance work over the Internet, my grander ambition had become to make a European sale of the book. The income, the prestige and the contacts that it could generate for future work seemed seductively real. Sure, I can be faulted for naively pinning too many hopes on him based on too little evidence. But hope is often the only thing that keeps a writer working. Hope propels you from page to page—hope that you can write the next word, hope that you can keep the reader involved, hope that pouring out your heart and your ideas will mean something to someone.

My hopes for *Echo Valley's* success diminished with each day that Terry Harris was silent. Finally, he resurfaced, responding to one of several e-mails:

```
Subject: Re: Anybody home?
Date: Thu, 20 Nov 1997 04:15:15
From: Terry Harris
To: Chris Westphal

Dear Chris,
Sorry about the silence. Life has been pretty hectic
and without any specifics to offer you, I saw little
point in telling you I was in the middle of things.
As you do know, the UK end of the business got into a
mess without me. I was trying to raise capital in the
US. I came back to England to see just what was going
on and what could be done.
After all the excitement, and there is still some of
this going on, it looks very much as if I will be back
behind my desk in NYC running HMR. Bruno Janlois, the
third corner of the partnership, is buying the
American operation and I will be running it. It will
take a few weeks for all the paperwork and legals to
go through but they are in progress now.
I am sorry that this has left you in limbo for a cou-
ple of months but there was little I could tell you
until I had some answers myself.
Regards
Terry
```

Less than confident that Terry Harris would meet his obligations—yet still willing to accept even the vague explanations above—I responded.

```
Subject: Re: Anybody home?
Date: Thu, 20 Nov 1997 14:45:25
From: Chris Westphal
To: Terry Harris

Dear Terry,
Good to hear from you after your long—and apparently
tumultuous—silence. I would like to receive the
remainder of the advance and take it from there.
Regards,
Chris
```

When Thanksgiving rolled around, we were invited to the home of Stephen and Leslie Malott. They had been in Prague only a few weeks longer than we, and on previous postings had lived in the Seychelles and India. Somehow—even though their furniture had only been delivered within the past couple of days—they were ready to entertain. To us, being invited to their home was like being rescued after a flood. We didn't care if we had to sit on packing crates and eat off paper plates, it would feel good to be in someone's home and to talk with others for more than the few minutes it took to have a cup of coffee and a cookie after church.

How about those Carrots?

In our zeal to cut down on the luggage we would bring, we hadn't brought our cookbooks, so I was left to depend on my faulty memory to come up with the recipe for the side dish we agreed to bring for Thanksgiving. "How about those carrots from the Ranch House?" Stephanie suggested. The Ranch House is a well-known vegetarian restaurant in Ojai, and we had bought one of their cookbooks just prior to our departure. The main ingredients in the dish were carrots and crushed pineapple, but it also contained cardamom.

Naturally, I only began the project the afternoon before dinner and had no idea what cardamom was in Czech. I found cinnamon, though. When the dish is made properly, the tangy cardamom spices up the bland carrots. The pineapple is a nice contrast—sweet and soft. The dish is also layered, and there is a specific sequence in which the ingredients are added. I didn't remember any of that. Instead, I just boiled the carrots for a while, dumped them in a bowl with the crushed pineapple, sprinkled in some cinnamon, and hoped for the best. We covered the dish tightly in foil. Not much of it spilled on the jostling metro and bus trip to Mala Sarka, a small enclave adjacent to ISP.

We had only passed by the neighborhood on our occasional visits by bus to ISP and had never been inside. As we entered, it was almost as though we were back on American soil. ISP financed the development, which is on property adjacent to the campus. The U.S. State Department owns half of the houses. We walked past the large homes and saw the manicured lawns and sturdy American cars in the driveways.

Stepping inside the Malott's home was like walking through a portal into a living room in the U.S. Even though they had just gotten most of their belongings, Leslie was already nearly finished decorating. On the walls and displayed elsewhere were art and artifacts from the various places they had lived and traveled. We knew we were in an American home, though, by the size of the refrigerator—a giant side-by-side that dwarfed the little ones seen in most European homes. Leslie had roasted a turkey and prepared all the trimmings, including fresh-baked biscuits. Rich aromas wafted through the house. The Krikavas were also there with their two children, Joe and Emily. William and Mary-Margaret, the Malott's two children, helped Leslie in the kitchen; then they went upstairs until dinner with the other children.

It was heavenly for Stephanie and me to be among friends with whom we shared the common experience of living abroad. During the meal, the conversation was lively and engaging as everyone explained how and why they were in Prague. The Malotts had both been academics and were married in their thirties. Somewhat as a lark, they took the Foreign Service exam, and Stephen was offered a position in the State Department. They still had a home in the U.S., but their children had grown up mostly in foreign countries.

Jim Krikava had come with his family right after the "Velvet Revolution" to work as a missionary. Jim's grandparents were Czech, but Jim had been brought up on a farm in the Midwest. He had visited the country as a child, but hadn't learned the language until he was an adult.

Then it was our turn. We explained how we had simply wanted to live abroad, having nothing so compelling as a posting nor so noble as a mission to draw us here. The others thought this was wonderfully brave of us and were doubly impressed when we told them that we had arrived only with what suitcases we could carry on the plane.

We told Leslie how surprised we were that she could host such an evening so soon after receiving her belongings from the U.S., and she dismissed the accomplishment as though it was nothing to unpack and arrange a houseful of furniture in a couple of days. At one point, Stephanie made a complimentary remark about the china and wondered how one packed such delicate items for shipment abroad.

"You just hope for the best," Leslie said. She then told the story of a conversation with a friend—also a veteran expat—who was appalled that Leslie brought her good china on her overseas postings at all. "Aren't you afraid it'll get broken?" the friend had asked. "Why don't you just pack it away at home?"

Leslie responded, "Because I want to use it as much as I can. This is my life." To the table, she said, "So that's my philosophy: use the good china."

Her anecdote was so apropos of our life in Prague that it gave me particular cause for thought. Yes, we had done this bold thing and moved to a new country, but we weren't living it to the fullest. Stuck in a panelak a million miles from everything, we were missing out on half of what was available to us.

After dinner, the children put on a skit for us, and as I watched my own children interacting with the others, I felt as though I had betrayed them. At school, they had an active day, full of engagement and friendship. But at home, exhausted, it was just us, Larry King, and *Scoobie Doo*. In short, the children's lives were not integrated as they should be.

We got a ride home that night—feeling like the poor relations—and as we went up to our apartment in the cramped and graffiti-scarred elevator, our sense of gloom that had lifted over dinner returned with a vengeance. Our bold and romantic adventure was turning into miserable drudgery.

As often as possible, we got out of the apartment, but with the hectic schedules of work and school, just going down the street to the local "Pizza Go Home" was a chore. We had come to Prague to avoid getting in a rut and had managed to dig one for ourselves anyway—just in a different part of the world.

Even out in public, we were still isolated. At the bus stop, Stephanie and I would constantly hush the children, not wanting them to advertise their American-ness. We didn't want anyone saying, "Oh, we saw an American child on the bus, and he was so loud and rude." The proprietress of the drink shop continued to stare at us suspiciously when we came through the lobby. The clerks at the Delvita Supermarket still didn't know who we were—or didn't seem to—even though we were there practically every day for something or other. In the U.S., they'd be calling us by our first names and bagging the groceries for us. Here, they called out the price total and barely said thanks.

Our situation was not unique to expatriates. We had reached that point where we knew we were not a part of this place, yet we hadn't yet found a group with which to ally ourselves.

Meanwhile, the Czech translation of *Echo Valley* was done, but Terry Harris had once again dropped off my radar, and I had lost my patience.

```
Subject: Foreign rights
Date: Wed, 26 Nov 1997 17:02:34
From: Chris Westphal
To: Terry Harris

Terry,
Having gotten no response from you regarding my
repeated request for the final payment of advance
monies due to me, I am wondering if you wish to main-
tain our contractual relationship at all. Per your
oral statements to me, I am proceeding with marketing
Czech translation rights with the express understand-
ing that all advances, royalties and other monies
earned in the Czech market belong 100% to me and that
you or your company have no claim to them. I am also
considering marketing other European translation
rights here, in that you are currently in violation of
the contract anyway and appear to have lost interest
in marketing the book at all, or in maintaining the
contract. Let me know as soon as possible your inten-
tions.
Chris
```

A Father Who Came in from the Cold

Several days after the Thanksgiving feast at the Malotts, Kelsey came down with a serious case of croup. She wheezed and coughed, and our usual remedies had little effect. Through Marie, we found an English-speaking doctor who had an office nearby.

I stayed home with Kelsey the following day. She lay listlessly on the couch, her eyes half opened, wheezing each breath while I half-heartedly worked over the Internet, researching and writing sports trivia questions for a multimedia game for my U.S. client. *Scoobie Doo* blared in the background. A half hour before the appointment, I bundled Kelsey up, double-checked the map, and headed to the bus stop. By my reckoning, we needed to travel only a few stops, then get off. According to the map, the office was just a couple of blocks away from the stop.

As we got off the bus, rain drizzled from a flannel gray sky. I carried Kelsey as I searched for the address. Her wet hair was lank on her forehead, and I could hear her strained breathing. I walked for more than an hour and a half with her, searching like an idiot for the doctor's office, tramping across sodden fields, across vacant lots, going up and down hills, and back and forth on the wrong streets. There wasn't a taxi in sight, or I would have risked life and limb to take one.

By the time we found the doctor's office, we'd missed the appointment, but the receptionist looked through the glass and, seeing such a forlorn pair, let us in.

Fortunately, there was still a doctor there, and she spoke excellent English. The examination took only a few minutes, and the doctor prescribed a decongestant and then asked general questions about Kelsey's health. Casually, she asked where Kelsey went to school, and when I told her ISP, her eyes widened. "How does she get there?"

"By taxi, with my son."

"But it must be an hour!"

"Sometimes more," I admitted.

The doctor gave me a stern Slavic glare. "That's too hard for her."

Sheepishly, I tried to explain that initially we had expected to send the children to the British School, just a few tram stops from our apartment, but suddenly all the reasons we had had for taking the apartment sounded like pathetic excuses. I felt like a criminal.

That night, we decided to take Leslie's philosophy to heart and spend our time in Prague living to the fullest. It was time to move.

The Shocking Truth about Culture Shock

On the scale of life changes, moving to another country is off the register. Shall we consider the stress of moving alone? Pile on top of that sending your children to new and entirely different schools, a new work environment, perhaps even an entirely new career, the isolation of being in a foreign country, and all the attendant hassles and aggravations of settling into a new culture, and you have a recipe for culture shock.

Culture shock is not a single event, but an unfolding series of them. Suddenly, everything is different: money, language, and social protocols. And culture shock can strike wherever you go. In fact, if you go to England, where they reportedly speak the same language, you may have a more difficult time adjusting than you would in, say, Japan. Why? Because in England you'll be more likely to expect things to be the same, and they won't be. For starters, they've got this thing about warm beer, they insist on calling the hood of a car the bonnet, and they still have a queen. In a more "exotic" country, you will be more psychologically prepared for things to be different and consequently have an easier time adjusting to them.

Wherever you go, you will to some degree or another go through a fairly predictable series of emotions as you adapt to life overseas. Here's what you can expect:

The honeymoon stage: You at first exist in a bubble of security and comfort that you brought with you from home. It was in your luggage somewhere. From this safe little bubble, everything outside is beautiful and new. *"This little hut is so cute—right out of a Tarzan movie. It'll be fun to skip down to the well every morning and get water. We'll get exercise, too! Carefree and unburdened by material concerns, the people are always smiling and happy. The food is plain but wholesome; the weather hot, still, and peaceful."* After four or five weeks, though, the charm wears off as you enter...

The hostile stage: *"If I have to haul one more drop of that foul tasting water up that hill, I'm gonna scream. Haven't these people ever heard of plumbing? You'd think that over the centuries, one of them would wipe that grin off his face and work just a little to improve conditions around here! They don't even change the menu; it's all plain and boring. It's no wonder, though, with weather that never dips below 90 degrees!"* For five or six weeks more, your hostile feelings build as you find example after example of incompetence, stupidity, and poor planning. Around the end of the third month, your emotions reach their nadir as you enter...

The Stress Stage: *"The people who first settled this god-forsaken wart on the planet have spawned a race of twittering nitwits. Their food tastes like library paste, but it doesn't even matter because who could possibly have any sort of appetite when you live in a sauna!"* Feeling unable to relate at all to the native culture, you may seek other expatriates exclusively—and spend your time complaining about the natives, the country, and the food. You may demonstrate physical signs of stress: overeating, drinking to excess, insomnia, and emotional outbursts. But eventually, after you've been in the country for four or five months, you'll reach...

The Adaptation Stage: *"Well, I'm not thrilled about hauling the water, but the exercise is good, and on cooler days, the food is delicious. The natives aren't really all that lazy, either; they just have a different set of priorities and don't let little things bother them. The weather's too warm for me, but it's nice to be able to wear shorts day and night."* At this point, you see the pluses and minuses of your new country and feel that you can deal with them, even if you don't really like them all the time.

Depression:

Are you depressed? The isolation of living abroad can exacerbate feelings of depression. The National Mental Health Association, on the Web at www.nmha.org, lists the following as symptoms of depression:

- A persistent sad, anxious or "empty" mood.
- Sleeping too little or sleeping too much.
- Reduced appetite and weight loss, or increased appetite and weight gain.
- Loss of interest or pleasure in activities once enjoyed.
- Restlessness or irritability.
- Persistent physical symptoms that don't respond to treatment (such as headaches, chronic pain, or constipation and other digestive disorders).
- Difficulty concentrating, remembering, or making decisions.
- Fatigue or loss of energy.
- Feeling guilty, hopeless, or worthless.
- Thoughts of death or suicide.

If you experience one or more of these symptoms for more than a couple of weeks, you may be clinically depressed. The good news is that clinical depression is highly treatable, both with therapy and with new medications that have few side effects. The NMHA's Web site offers a quick "screening test" that, while not a formal diagnostic tool, will help you determine if you're depressed. The site also features links that will aid you in finding discussion groups, help, and further information about depression. Another site worth looking at is the Depression Alliance, a U.K. charity devoted to helping people cope with and remedy depression, on the Web at www.depressionalliance.org.

Reducing Culture Shock

Much of what we consider culture shock is our own unwillingness or inability to accept the fact that the way we do things at home isn't necessarily the "right" way and is definitely not the only way. It is just one of the ways. If nothing else, living abroad gives you an opportunity to see that there are many ways to live in this world and that each of them has its own integrity. We were amazed in Prague, for example, at how many stamps the immigration officials had to put on our residency forms. They had whole trees of stamps on their desks, and each one had its role. We could have gotten worked up about it or complained about the inefficiency of the system, but for the most part (not always), we just found it entertaining.

Here are a few ways to reduce your susceptibility to culture shock:

- Learn as much as you can about the country's history and culture. For us, the fact that the Czech Republic has been dominated and frequently betrayed by more powerful forces—the Austro-Hungarian Empire, the Germans, and then the Soviet Union—explained a lot of what we viewed as the people's "suspicious" nature. Once we got to know some Czechs, we found them exceedingly warm and generous.

- Don't even bother thinking about "how it's done back home." This isn't back home.

- When something, such as bureaucracy or inefficiency, gets to be overwhelming, try looking at it as would an objective observer. Set your emotions aside for the moment, and just do what needs to be done. You can yell and scream when it's all over.

- Try to get to know natives of the country. If help is offered, accept it graciously and reciprocate. Having acquaintances in the country will help you feel less isolated.

- Don't hang out with expatriates who complain about the people, the conditions, or the customs. It will only make you more resistant to adapting to the culture. Occasionally venting your frustrations with others is good and will keep you from blowing up at those around you, but try not to dwell on those things.

- Socialize with expatriates who like and understand the country you're in. In Prague, many of the people whom we became closest to were Czechs who had fled the country after the 1968 Warsaw Pact invasion and then returned after the 1989 Velvet Revolution. They had a keen understanding of the country and were eager to share it with us.

Expat Answers: *What can expatriate families do to address feelings of loneliness and isolation?*

- *Be aware that these feelings will come and that they are part of the adjustment process. They will also pass!*

- *Take the initiative and look for local resources and groups who deal specifically with expatriates.*

- *Keep in contact with relatives from home who are supportive of the move.*

- *Don't isolate yourself from the people in your community.*

- *NEVER rely entirely on communication with home friends—it makes things worse.*

- *Learn the local culture and scene.*

- *Learn at least some basic phrases in the local language.*

- *Study and become an expert in some aspect of the local scene—history is a good bet.*

- *Make the most of the school breaks by traveling and changing scenery. If possible, consider an annual trip home.*

–Various respondents

SIX

'Carp' Diem

"You know you're an expat when... you aren't able to go home for important family events due to the expense of travel."

—Danielle Surkatty, Indonesia

Now that we knew our way around Prague, it was easy to identify the general area where we wanted to live: Prague 6. Other than the center, Prague 6 is the most expensive part of the city and is home to most of the embassies and consulates, as well as the majority of the diplomatic personnel. Of course, it was also home to ISP, and that was one of its major attractions to us.

I asked the school's director, David Buck, if he could recommend a broker or an agent of some kind who could help out with our apartment search. David gave me a business card for an agent named Michael Rones. He said several other expats had been happy with Michael's services.

We spoke with Michael a few times on the telephone, then took the metro out to Prague 6, where we met him at the first of several apartments he had arranged for us to see. It was a panelak, though a slightly newer version than the one we were living in. It had been totally renovated, and everything was new, including the furniture, which was mostly finished with black lacquer. That, along with the white carpet, made the place look more like a swinging bachelor pad than a family home. It was only nominally larger than our current apartment, yet twice as expensive.

Over the next several days, we rode in Michael's battered Skoda to see some truly bizarre apartments furnished with broken down furniture and hopeless carpet. Color schemes favored the more putrid shades of orange, green, and brown. We figured that we might be stuck out in Modrany after all, or that we would take the bachelor pad and at least be closer to ISP. Nothing seemed too promising.

Then Michael took us to an apartment that was still in the midst of renovation. It occupied the third floor and attic of a 1913 Art Nouveau tri-plex on a narrow cobbled street. A small business occupied the ground floor, and there was another apartment on the second floor. The hardwood floors were still being installed, but already it was by far the best place we had seen. The large living room had a corner fireplace, a grand piano, art nouveau light fixtures, and an antique china cabinet with inlaid wood. Hanging on the walls were prints of work by Gustav Klimt, one of Stephanie's favorite artists. We were certain that this place was way out of our price range.

The Kind of Place We Had Envisioned

But it was only $1,200—twice what we were paying, but the same as the bachelor pad. And this place was huge, with two bathrooms, three bedrooms, and a nice terraced yard. Best of all, it was only a 10 minute drive to ISP. We desperately wanted it and told Michael we'd wait however long it took to finish the renovations.

Just as we were leaving, the owner's wife, Hanna Cernikova, arrived with her new baby, Bart[5], to oversee the workmen. Even though she spoke very little English, we immediately liked her. In broken Czech, we told her how much we loved the apartment. "Je moc krasny!"[6] I enthused, and complimented her on all the improvements she had made.

Though some others had seen the apartment earlier, it was apparently this meeting with Hanna that had made the difference for us. Michael called us that night, saying that we had gotten it. Finally, Drew and Kelsey would be able to have friends over! Besides being able to sleep in a little in the mornings, we promised them frequent sleepovers, birthday parties—everything they had been missing so stoically for the previous four months.

We knew that life would be dramatically better in our new home, and our moods were buoyed tremendously by the prospects ahead. This was the type of place we had envisioned at the start—distinctive, charming, and

---

[5]Named in honor of Bart Simpson. Honest.
[6]"It's very pretty."

in a good location. I would have been thrilled to have this apartment in any city in the world.

Needless to say, our current landlady, Marie, wasn't overjoyed to hear the news that we were moving. I told her that, while her apartment was all that we could have wanted, the location was simply too inconvenient. She said she understood, but took pains to point out that we had a lease. What were we going to do about that?

I couldn't possibly afford to pay for both apartments. I offered to pay her two months rent—January and February—even though we would move out in mid-December, and she begrudgingly agreed. We doubted Marie would cause us any more trouble, but just the same, we made sure that the apartment was left in absolutely spotless condition, which included for Stephanie almost an entire day devoted to ironing the linens.

Finally, when moving day arrived, all of our possessions fit into a single rented van, something I haven't been able to accomplish since college. The whole move took an hour and a half, with the only glitch being that we accidentally left Stephanie's beloved laundry rack behind in the lobby. Via tram, subway, and bus, I made it back to the building, but someone had helped himself to it.

In any case, we were fairly well unpacked at our new place by the end of the weekend. In the larger bedroom, a ship's ladder led up to a loft, which Kelsey claimed as her bedroom. Drew took the bottom part of the room. The living room had large windows that opened onto a balcony overlooking a park across the street. The trees were bare now, but in the spring it would be a great place for the children to play. Just down the street was a convent, and from time to time we'd see the habited sisters

TIP: Corporations usually pay a lot more for housing than ordinary residents, and relocation services typically charge a month or more in rent to find you a place. You'll save a lot of money searching for yourself and networking with other expats to find a house or apartment.

 TIP: Remember when the U.S. had something called the Phone Company? Telephone service still seems to be a monopoly in much of Europe, and if an apartment doesn't have a phone, it may take you months to get one. Save yourself the aggravation and make sure that any apartment or house you rent already has an operating phone.

strolling past our door, a vision from an old Europe that somehow had survived all the battering of progress.

Meanwhile, I was still working hard on making a European sale of *Echo Valley*, even amid all the tumult and unhappiness of November. The translated sections were now finished, and my Czech agent, Kristen Olsen, was sending them off. Before we moved, I solicited advice from my friend, Scott.

Subject:Translation of Echo Valley
Date: Tue, 25 Nov 1997 08:17
From: Chris Westphal
To: Scott White

Dear Scott,
 I got my Czech translation of a section of *Echo Valley*. It looks good, but that's as far as I can go. Does this sound right to you: "Takovy krasny den, pomyslel si Tom pri ceste domu. Jak se blizil k Los Angeles, provoz na dalnici stale houstnul." Does it have the zing of the original? Could we maybe mix these words up a little, say, longer words at the beginning, and going downward? Should we alphabetize the words? Your thoughts.
Chris

Subject: Re: Translation
Date: Wed, 26 Nov 1997 15:08:57
From: Scott White
To: Chris Westphal

Dear Chris,
The translation of *Echo Valley* looks OK. A bit lacking the same dynamic inflections perhaps, but considering the target audience, go for it. I couldn't help but notice the obvious mistake in verb conjugation in the third sentence—I believe the possessive past tense of the verb "blazil" should be 'blazeep'... its a little thing, but if it were my work being raped that way, well... I do like the idea of arranging the words by size, but perhaps go from smallest to largest - let the reader work up to 4-5 syllable jobs with no conso- nants. What do you think?
Scott

Subject: Linguistics
Date: Thu, 27 Nov 1997 09:41:22
From: Chris Westphal
To: Scott White

Dear Scott,
Your astute linguistic observations regarding the
Czech version of *Echo Valley* were most welcome. I have
duly passed them along to the translator, along with a
stinging rebuke. I wrote it in iambic pentameter, and
then alphabetized every fourth word, starting with the
letter "M" and skipping randomly backwards and for-
wards in the alphabet. The effect was utterly pleasing
from an aesthetic point of view, but I'm afraid the
meaning might have suffered somewhat. Such are the
rewards and perils of scholarship.
-Chris

ISP's Christmas break was to begin soon after we moved into the new apartment, but the children were eager to take us up on our vow that they could have lots of play dates. Finally, we would get a chance to spend some time with the friends they had been telling us about since September. At ISP, their social sphere was broader than it had ever been. Drew's best friend was Aaron Bata, whose father was an attorney who had his own firm with offices in Prague and Budapest and had been born in Hungary. Aaron had lived most of his life in Manhattan and even had a regular role on a popular network TV show as a child. He and Drew were inseparable, and it wasn't long before they were regularly taking taxis from one home to the other.

A Veritable United Nations

Kelsey's closest friends were Milena Paprok—the girl whose family she had sat with at the circus—and Kim Najman. Milena was the daughter of Michael Paprok, who was Czech but had lived in Canada and the U.S. for more than 20 years. Her mother was Young-Joo, from Korea. Kim's father, Jaroslav, was also Czech. He had left what was then Czechoslovakia in 1968 and immigrated to Sweden. Working in Indonesia, he met his wife, Nancy, who was Dutch.

By knowing these children whose own families were a veritable United Nations, and of course many other classmates, Drew and Kelsey gained an invaluable glimpse of other cultures. Expatriate children,

MORE DATA, PLEASE... A good place to start on your overseas house hunt is DirectMoving.com, on the Web at www.directmoving.com. Click on Recommended sites/Housing. There, you'll find links to dozens of overseas and domestic house finding services, plus a vast amount of other information and links.

MORE DATA, PLEASE... To quickly find the embassy of a country you hope to visit, try The Embassy Network at www.emb.com.

accustomed to being "the new kid" themselves, had immediately embraced our children. The ready acceptance by their classmates went a long way in alleviating Drew and Kelsey's occasional homesickness. Early on, Kelsey had drawn pictures showing Ojai and the friends who she missed back home. On these illustrations, in bold letters, she would write things such as "Ojai RULES!"

Drew often wrote to friends back home and was disappointed that they seldom responded. We explained that he had a greater desire to communicate because he was doing something that was so different from his ordinary life. He understood, but it still hurt his feelings that he received so few letters or e-mails. Still, in many ways, though he did miss his friends back home, he was having the best year of his life. He had been elected his class's student council representative and was chosen to sing a solo at the school's Christmas program. I was enormously proud of both of them and thought that I, certainly, could learn a lesson or two from both about how to adapt to change.

Even though Christmas was just around the corner, neither Drew nor Kelsey seemed to miss California, and Stephanie and I were determined to make Christmas in Prague as "homey" as possible. A day or so after moving in, we had bought a Christmas tree, hauling it home in a taxi. We made ornaments and sent Christmas cards. We even managed to host a Christmas party, inviting Eva and her family, plus friends from ISP and the Caledonian. As we shared some Christmas cheer, I was taken with how far we had actually come. We had arrived in the country knowing only Eva, and now we had a houseful of people, and the children were playing upstairs with their own friends. I was proud of myself and of Stephanie for what we had accomplished, too. Living abroad was the most dramatic test of our marriage. It takes a tremendous amount of teamwork to move to another country, and though we had had our disagreements, overall we recognized that each of us brought different strengths to the marriage.

Like me, Stephanie is also a writer and had a romance novel published in 1995. With her now working as a teacher, her life and the family dynamics had changed; since we'd been married in 1984, Stephanie had never worked outside the home. Here in Prague, I had necessarily taken on more of a domestic role. This made me unusual among the expatriate families we'd gotten to know—and I confess that I wasn't always jolly about it or about my frustrating work situation. Among the men, I sometimes felt like odd man out, as most husbands were executives or diplomats of one sort or another. But not all.

Expatriate families come in all shapes and sizes. The Papirniks, friends we got to know months later, were both Czech but had lived in the U.S. for a number of years. Rudolph was a stockbroker back home, and his wife, Val, was a lawyer. In Prague, Val worked full-time at a law firm, and Rudolph looked after their three children and did some day trading in the stock market. Another couple, whom we knew only tangentially, had an arrangement similar to ours—the wife worked at Radio Free Europe, while the husband was a freelance writer.

What seemed to hold together our family and the others was shared values and shared interests. Successful expatriates are, as one would expect, open to new cultures and eager to try new things—whether that means learning a new language, new customs, or new family dynamics. Sometime earlier, Peggy Krikava and I had discussed what kinds of things make expatriate families different. Most notably, expat families are closer knit than others. They have to be, she said, because the stresses and strains of life outside of one's native country are hard on a marriage.

According to Peggy, only one in seven Americans can successfully leave the U.S. and have a good experience in another country, regardless of the country. Having met a lot of expatriates through ISP and through the church, it was her opinion that families chosen for international postings are usually a lot stronger than average.

Real Life Takes a Holiday

Certainly, I think our family was stronger because of our experience abroad. We necessarily depended more on one another than we ever had. Still, Stephanie and I managed to find time for a huge fight a few days after moving into the new apartment. The topic was "Should we stay for more than a year?" Stephanie—enjoying urban life and feeling that the new apartment would make everything much easier—took the affirmative. I—still coping with my goofy publisher and feeling isolated because of my work situation—took the negative.

The setting was a small coffee house, Gulu Gulu, tucked along the labyrinthine streets adjacent to Narodni Trida. The place was filled with 20-something hipsters, both Czech and expatriate, and under other circumstances, we would have been reveling in their reflected youth and freedom. The walls were covered with art. The place was full of conversation, laughter, and smoke. But Stephanie and I were creating our own atmosphere, brittle with tension.

"What does Prague have to do with our real life?" I asked. "Where is it going to take us?"

"I don't know," she said. "But I really like it here."

She railed against the smallness of Ojai, a town where it's virtually impossible to go to the supermarket without running into someone you know. She liked the opportunity to re-invent herself somewhere new. I, on the other hand, liked Ojai, where for the first time in my life I'd been active in community affairs and—best of all—found a lot of other friends who were artists and writers. Stephanie liked that element, too, but now urban anonymity outweighed it.

"I agreed to a year," I said.

"Well, I might want to make it longer. We did it your way. We came. So am I just supposed to follow you around?"

I had no answer. So I stormed out of the café. (Note to self: This is a very stupid thing to do.)

Christmas was coming. Neither of us wanted to fight. We patched things up, agreeing that in a few months we'd objectively re-examine the idea of staying on. A few days later, we were friends again. We were walking on the ancient Charles Bridge, which crosses the Vltava River and connects the Mala Strana, "Little Street," and Stare Mesto, "Old Town," districts of the city. In August, when we had arrived, the bridge was teeming with tourists, and vendors were hawking everything from line drawings to jester's hats to cheap marionettes. Now it was virtually deserted.

The bridge is lined with graceful sandstone statues depicting various saints. High up on a hill overlooking the city, the jagged spires of the St. Vitus Cathedral at the castle were silhouetted against the sky, and the lights of the city glistened in the slowly moving river. "I couldn't stand it a few days ago, but right now I think this is the best thing we've ever done," I said. No wonder my wife wants to kill me sometimes.

Yes, we had a ticket on an emotional roller coaster. Emotional ups and downs are part and parcel of living in a new country. You're constantly bombarded by new stimuli, new challenges. You see yourself and those around you in different lights—not all of them flattering.

We stopped and drank in the majestic view.

"This was a bold thing to do," she said.

"Definitely," I agreed. "And kind of insane."

For the moment, both of us seemed to feel that we were living in a dream realized. We couldn't believe that we'd already been in Prague almost five months. I still wasn't in any mood to consider staying beyond a year, but I had to admit that, difficulties aside, this had been a hell of an adventure so far.

"It's only a year," Stephanie said.

"I know. It'll go so fast. And when we're back home, we'll remember it and it'll probably be hard to believe we really did it."

"But we did," she said.

```
Subject: Strange, strange, strange
Date: Fri, 05 Dec 1997 08:39:50 +0100
From: Chris Westphal
To: Cynthia Kear & Gordon Skene

Dear Cynthia & Gordon,
Well, of course no word from his Terriness. I tried
his number in England, which just rings. Then I tried
his number in New York. The first time, a phone compa-
ny recording referred me to a fax. Yesterday, however,
the recording gave me a new number. I thought Terry
might have gotten a new line that he'll actually
answer. Unfortunately, it rings through to a scratchy
recording for some bogus corporation or other.
No hint of Terry or of any relation to publishing of
any kind.
If you're in the mood for punishment, you might try
it:
212.414.1788.
The answer is something like "Bona Fabula,
```

Incorporated."
Now, if it was "Bonton Confabulation," maybe I would
think it was some clever witticism on Terry's part
(though I would be over-stating his cleverness and
wittiness). To me, Bona Fabula (if that's it; it's
hardly coherent) sounds like some kind of bone. I
guess that's fibula.
Anyway, any news, thoughts, observations or just plain
ranting and raving would be welcomed in this quarter.
We're all in the same boat, and a leaky craft it is
with Terry nominally at the helm, though he seems to
have abandoned ship.
Later,
Chris Westphal

Looking back on our early experience, I realize how eager I was to punish myself when things didn't work out as I had hoped. I berated myself because Terry Harris was such a flake. I gave myself no mercy for hurriedly choosing the first apartment. I was disgusted that I hadn't been able to find a better work situation, when in actuality, working at home was often the only practical thing to do in light of my family responsibilities. But any failure or disappointment—and there were plenty to go around—would arouse in me an almost vicious need to second-guess absolutely every decision I had made up to that point. If only I could learn to be as wise and compassionate with myself as I am with my children.

Initially, as we left for Prague, Stephanie and I had told the children to look at each day and each new experience as a lesson. "Some things will seem strange," we said. "but just experience them and realize that you're seeing something different and new in your life. Try and appreciate it... or just laugh at it."

I couldn't—or didn't—always take my own advice, but I tried. Especially during Christmas, it's impossible to focus on mistakes. Prague just before Christmas inspires a joyous kind of innocent wonder. The city absolutely sparkled with vitality. Festive booths on Old Town Square sold handicrafts, hot mulled wine, and of course, excellent Czech beer. On the winding streets of Old Town itself, hand-painted eggs, marionettes, and other crafts were for sale. There was a warmth to the city, even in the chill of winter, that couldn't help but brighten one's mood.

At night, trios of costumed men roamed the streets. One was dressed in the flowing robes of Saint Michael. Another wore angel garb, and the third was the devil. They approach young children and asked them if they'd been good. Of course, the children, their voices quivering, answered, "Yes," and were rewarded with candy.

The trio typically then headed to the nearest hospoda, or pub, where they were usually welcomed with free drinks. As a result, by 9:00, most of the costumed trios were roaring drunk.

Since there were few tourists at this time of year, we felt like we were a part of the city and had been given a special glimpse into the life of it. Most of the Czech traditions—the beautiful carols playing in the stores, the strolling carolers—we could easily understand. But not all of them.

> Subject: Where are you, and why don't you answer your phone??
> Date: Fri, 05 Dec 1997 08:48:27
> From: Chris Westphal
> To: Terry Harris
>
> I am losing my patience.
> -Chris Westphal

Just a few days before Christmas, large blue plastic tubs began appearing on the street corners all over the city.

Passing by them, I figured they were part of some municipal program for collecting trash or toys for the poor. Then on the following day, all of the tubs were filled with water, and swimming in the water were fat carp.

They were being sold for the Christmas feast—a tradition for Czechs that dates back to the fourteenth century, when the fish were raised in huge ponds for royal banquets and considered a rare delicacy. The upper classes jumped on the carp bandwagon. However, carp grow and multiply quickly, so before long there were too many for the upper classes to consume, and it became obligatory for the lower class to eat them, too—so much so that the lower class begged to have carp only once a week.

But everyone's still pretty geared up about carp just before Christmas. Families will peer into the tubs and select a fish, then take it home in a water-filled plastic bag. Then, until Christmas Eve, it will live in the bathtub, doted on by the children and probably resented by the adults, who can't take a bath.

Czechs who we asked about this tradition said that by the time the fateful night arrived, the children had usually adopted the carp as a pet.

So it's a heart-rending struggle between appetite and affection. Affection often wins out, and thousands of the fish are given a reprieve, let loose in the Vltava River which snakes like a question mark through Prague.

To avoid the trauma caused by the eating of a beloved pet, the fishmongers will also butcher the carp on the spot, if requested. No one gets too emotionally attached to filets. We would watch the fishmongers as people selected their prize, then stand by as it was butchered. "Gross," said Kelsey.

Though it is a very secular country, Christmas in the Czech Republic is still a magical time, and it seems to have been considerably less commercialized than it is in the U.S. Being there at that time was wonderful because we knew that none of this was done for the sake of tourism, and we were privileged to partake of it. That, and other moments like it, is one thing that makes expatriate life special and memorable.

But that still left the matter of what to have for Christmas Eve dinner. "We don't have to have carp, do we?" Kelsey wanted to know. "Well, as the saying goes, 'When in Rome, do as the Romans do.'" "Dad, we're in Prague." "True." We had pizza.

House Hunting Hell

As the old saying goes, there are three important things in real estate: location, location, and location. But how do you find the best place for your family to live when you don't even know your way around the city?

Our first apartment was a big mistake, and in hindsight, we were too hasty in choosing it, but we were too worried, too tired, and too sick of living out of suitcases to look anymore.

We had success in using a real estate agent recommended to us by the director of the ISP. See Chapter Six for a more thorough narrative about that successful venture.

The greatest assets in finding a good place to live are patience, luck, and money. A lot of any of them can compensate for a lack of any of the other two. Be aware that, in many countries, an apartment that meets western standards in terms of size and amenities may be a rare commodity, and consequently, much higher in price. Landlords in developing countries sometimes see westerners—particularly Americans—as easy targets; watch out for rent gouging. Depend upon the knowledge and experience of other expatriates or your agent to protect you.

Making Contact

Moving to another country on your own is not unlike being involved in organized crime or finding a job—networking is essential. To make it easier for you to find a house in your new country, before departure:

- Get maps and tourist guides.

- Call the embassy representing the country where you intend to go. You'll need to do this anyway to learn the residency requirements, so while you're at it, ask in which areas of the city you should focus your housing hunt.

- Contact the U.S. Embassy nearest your destination and ask for information on expatriates living in that country. What areas do they favor? To which schools do most send their children? What can you expect to pay for accommodations?

Once you've arrived,

- Network at the children's school, both with parents and staff. Most expats have been in the same boat and are eager to help.

- U.S. Embassies often have newsletters and bulletin boards. See if you can place an ad.

- Post notices at your children's school and at places frequented by expatriates.

- Contact the American Chamber of Commerce or similar organization.

- Read the ads in the local English language newspaper, and place an ad. If you know the language, use the local publications.

- Find an English language service organization, such as a church, synagogue, temple, the Rotary, etc., and get to know the others who are involved.

Tollhouse Cookies and Tortillas

When Stephanie interviewed for her job with the Caledonian School in Prague, she asked the director, "What's the most important single thing to bring to Prague?"

He answered, "A flexible attitude." This answer applies to any country you may choose.

Depending on your destination and your budget, the adjustments you make in living arrangements may be minor or dramatic. Corporate executives often live in separate expatriate neighborhoods, some of which look like they were uprooted from Southern California and planted on foreign soil. We lived in Czech neighborhoods and liked the variety of experience this provided.

Still, as is the case with many veteran expats, much of our social life centered around ISP. Often, living as an expat, especially in a non-English-speaking country, is like being on a life raft. Not everyone—perhaps not even the majority—will be American. But since English is the language of business, most people will typically share with you the common bond of language, and perhaps much more as well.

Immersion in the foreign culture is the entire point, of course. However, it's nice to be able to find someone who has a good recipe for toll-house cookies, or a connection to get tortillas, or who can help you deal with the frustrations of daily life in an unfamiliar place.

Expat Answers: *What simple advice would you give to expatriates when it comes to finding housing?*

- *Stay in a hotel/guesthouse at first and drive around the areas you like the look of to see what's available.*

- *Hire an independent advisor recommended by other expats. It's the best investment you'll ever make.*

- *Don't look at price as much as location, accessibility to shopping, and a quiet neighborhood.*

- *Consult an expat Web site and other expats.*

- *Don't think of your housing as temporary.*

- *Take your time.*

- *Let the spouse who is going to spend the most time at home choose the house.*

- *Find other foreigners and jump in on the newly vacated homes of those leaving.*

–Various respondents

SEVEN

Flying the Coop

We briefly considered going home for Christmas, but somehow that seemed like cheating. And it wasn't as though we'd never seen California at Christmas before. Back in October, anticipating a cold and gloomy winter, we thought ahead. Wouldn't some sunshine be nice? Where did Czechs go during winter, we wondered.

We asked Marie, who said that back in the "workers paradise" days, the dream destination for Czechs was Cuba, but now a lot of Czechs prefer the Canary Islands. That sounded just right to us. She recommended a travel agency called Fischer Travel, which sold complete vacation packages and had an office in central Prague.

Just arranging the trip was an adventure in itself.

```
Subject: Status?
Date: Sat, 3 Jan 1998 22:51:22 EST
From: Cynthia Kear
To: Chris Westphal

Chris,
Season's greetings.
Just thought I would check in & see what &/or if
you've heard anything from Mr. T.
He & I had some discussion mid Dec but he's gone
underground again. Anything shaking?
Well, here's to a better new year....
Best,
Cynthia
```

TIP: You may not have the e-mail addresses of friends at home who you see on a day-to-day basis. Make a special point of getting those addresses before you leave.

MORE DATA, PLEASE... Kallback, the originator of the callback international calling system, is on the Web at www.kallback.com. Kallback, 417 2nd Avenue W., Seattle, WA 98119, Tel: (Toll-free in the U.S.) 800.516.9992, Tel: (International) +206.479.8600, Fax: (Toll-free in the U.S.) 800.516.9993, Fax: (International) +206.479.0009, E-mail: info@kallback.com

I made several trips to the Fischer office where the crisply uniformed associates did their best to understand my Czech, and I did my best to understand their English. I came home with several fat, glossy books, one for each of the islands. Naturally, everything was written in Czech. Marie gave us some help figuring out the various symbols in each of the books that indicated things such as whether there were children's programs, whether meals were included, and whether or not there was a beach nearby. We picked a four-star, all-inclusive package to Lanzarote and hoped that the photo, showing a huge pool area surrounded by deck chairs and umbrellas, was accurate. Total cost for the four of us was a little more than $3,000 for the week—payable in cash or via a bank transfer.

I'd tried to arrange a couple of bank transfers to pay ISP tuition in the past, but it was an ordeal that involved multiple faxes, e-mails, and phone calls to my accountant in the U.S. I decided that cash was the more desirable option. Komercni Banka, just across the street from Fischer Travel's office, had a foreign exchange window. I just gave them my passport and was able to write them a check, with the funds guaranteed by my credit card.

The trip was the big Christmas present for everyone, but that still didn't stop Stephanie and me from buying too much stuff for the children. The big ticket items were a Czech puppet theater, plus marionettes for Kelsey and a big Lego helicopter for Drew. There was also the usual assortment of toys—electronic Gameboys, Tomagotchi "electronic" pets, books, and clothes, plus a few things shipped to us from my mother and a couple of friends. After the usual package-opening frenzy in the morning, we called family and friends back home, then went to one of the big downtown hotels for a brunch with the Paproks. All in all, it was a splendid Christmas, and a few days later we were headed for the airport.

"What's Lanzarote like?" Drew and Kelsey wanted to know.

"A little like Hawaii," we told them. That's what we thought.

```
Subject: Re: Status?
Date: Sun, 04 Jan 1998 19:36:02
From: Chris Westphal
To: Cynthia Kear

Absolutely nothing from Mr. T. I'm looking for
European agents. If I make any progress I'll let him
find me. If he turns up in the meantime with anything
meaningful, I'll listen to him.
Best,
Chris Westphal
```

"It looks like the moon," observed Stephanie as our bus wended through the bleak landscape of Lanzarote on the way from the airport to the hotel. The island, we soon learned, is essentially a chunk of pumice a couple of hundred miles off the Moroccan coast. The largest crops are lichen (some 250 varieties) and an insect, cochineals, which thrive on cactus and are crushed for the intense red pigment derived from their shiny red wings. Red lipstick? The color probably comes from these critters.

We had been the only non-Czechs on the plane, and as near as we could tell, we were the only Americans in the hotel, too. The registration form didn't even list the U.S. as a country of origin. But being outnumbered was by then nothing new for us, after five months in Prague. We'd become seasoned people-watchers, and the lobby was like a scene out of *Casablanca*. A group of Moroccan aristocrats, wearing long kaf-

TIP: You can usually cash a check at a bank that deals with foreign exchange. You have to show your passport and have a credit card to guarantee the funds, but it's fairly painless. American Express will also cash the personal checks of cardholders—giving you dollars or virtually any other currency. The exchange rate is usually abysmal, though.

TIP: Cash has one disadvantage: pickpockets. To protect yourself, keep your wallet in a front pocket or inside jacket pocket. Women should keep purses buckled and held under their arm—not flapping behind them. Conceal cameras and other things that mark you as a visitor. Pickpockets often work in teams, so if you're being pushed and shoved onto a bus or tram, beware: someone is probably trying to distract you so a partner can pick your pocket.

tans, strolled through the reception area while German, Italian, and Czech tourists listened to orientations in their native languages. As the islands are a part of Spain, the locals speak Castilian Spanish, so the effect was a swirling mix of tones and inflections. Fortunately, the desk clerk spoke English.

After settling in our room, we found the much-vaunted Youth Program in one of the hotel's two ballrooms. There, a gangly guy wearing a garish clown outfit was teaching a bunch of bored looking children a dance that looked like the Hokey Pokey.

"No way," said Drew. We agreed. Both children already did an admirable Hokey Pokey. Watching him, the idea of having the kids involved in fun activities while Stephanie and I enjoyed some adult time was quickly abandoned. But everything got better from there. We saw the sun for the first time in two months and enjoyed a buffet that included mountains of fresh fruits and vegetables and about five kinds of fish from the surrounding waters.

We actually spent little time at the hotel; we rented a little sedan and toured the island. Soon, we fell in love with its stark beauty.

We rode camels across the vast black sands, visited a pristine beach where—to the children's revulsion—many of the sunbathers were nude, and toured the tranquil grottos of Los Jameos del Agua (the water tubes), a huge network of volcanic caves where the island's inhabitants once hid from pirates and invaders.

```
Subject: Kudos on your kudos
Date: Mon, 05 Jan 1998 19:35:54
From: Chris Westphal
To: Annie Reeves
```

Dear Annie,
Hope you're well and dry in Ojai. We're recovering
from Phase III of culture shock. That is, we just
accept that we don't understand anything that's going
on around us. Today I got on three separate trams
that, judging from previous times I've been on them
and by their schedule, should have taken me to my destination. But NOOOOOO! Headed the wrong way. You kinda
take that stuff in stride after a while...

Isn't It a Little... Inappropriate?

We usually returned to the hotel for meals, and as New Year's Eve approached, we figured we'd stay at the hotel where a fireworks show and a party were planned. But that wasn't all. The hotel was also staging a production of *The Rocky Horror Show*. I thought we should go see it.

"Isn't it a little... inappropriate?" Stephanie asked cautiously.

It had been at least 20 years since I'd seen the film, which has been cult classic of midnight movies since the '70s. All I remembered was some trashy lingerie and some good rock tunes. "It is a family hotel," I said. "How bad can it be?"

My question was soon answered. We found a cocktail table in the small ballroom, where a stage had been set up. As a group of toddlers and pre-schoolers sat on the floor in front of the stage, I felt somewhat reassured. Surely, other guests—who could read the brochures and talk to the staff—had a better idea of what was in store, and they had brought children even younger than ours, so this would be okay.

TIP: Make sure you can download your credit card transactions onto your computer via the Internet. Contact the credit card issuer for instructions.

MORE DATA, PLEASE...
Find which credit cards offer the best rates by going on-line to www.bankrate.com.

```
Subject: Re: How are you guys?
Date: Mon, 12 Jan 1998 08:47:32
From: Chris Westphal
To: Sara Sackner

My PR stuff here is dribbling in, but I admit to lit-
tle enthusiasm for it. In the grand scheme of things,
it's got little to do with my overall interests, which
are (well, let's be honest) being a famous, fabulously
successful fiction writer. PR is a lot of fiction,
true, but I don't want to be famous for that. I
thought I'd title my next book, "Excuse Me, But I
Thought I Was Supposed to Be Famous."
Anyway, hope this finds you all well.
Love backatcha,
CW
```

MORE DATA, PLEASE...

An excellent currency converter is on the Web at Oanda.com. Depending upon the country, ex-change rates can fluctuate dramatically, and keeping an eye on them can result in considerable savings. www.oanda.com/cgi-bin/ncc.

The lights dimmed and the movie soundtrack thundered from huge speakers. Then the cast—made up of the hotel staff—emerged. As does the movie, the show started out like a campy horror picture. Unfortunately—also like the movie—it then became a moderately provocative burlesque.

As they donned outfits that could have come out of a Fredericks of Hollywood catalog, the hotel staff, which before had looked so proper in their crisp uniforms, revealed an entirely different side of their personalities. The star was none other than the gangly clown we had seen on the first day. He had swapped his baggy polka-dotted clown garb for a tight-fitting teddy and some wicked black heels. I knew there was something odd about him.

The toddlers gaped in open wonder as the plump waitress from dinner—bulging out of a skimpy French maid's uniform—leaped clumsily around, always a half-beat behind the pounding music. For more than an hour, in a total miscarriage of choreography, the cast careened about the stage while lip-synching to the soundtrack. True, they did pour a lot of energy into their performance, but since none of them spoke English, it was a little like watching a badly dubbed movie.

Stephanie and I were still stunned later as we watched a fireworks display, then celebrated the New Year's countdown with the children. Everyone put on party hats and blew noisemakers as we welcomed the New Year in this most unusual place in this most unusual year.

```
Subject:Re: the Czech way
Date: Wed, 28 Jan 1998 17:19:
From: Chris Westphal
To: J.B. White

J.B. wrote:

>Meanwhile, bundle up. It's about to get cold over
there.

JB:
Hey, it's late in coming, but you're damn right, old
sport. Big flat flakes. But enough about tourists; it
was snowing today!
It started with perfect little crystals that looked
like kids' patterned drawings of snowflakes. On a
black jacket (all I ever wear now is black. Not
because I like it, but because it's all I have) they
were little, well, snowflakes. Asterisks? Anyway, soon
it was slashing across the sky. About an inch an hour.
Stephanie and I walked across the Vltava (hey, this is
romantic, eh?). Well, I should say we walked across a
bridge over the Vltava, although there were sheets of
ice visible in the venerable river.
We enjoyed a couple of Irish Coffees at the Cafe
Savoy, along with some very fine crepes, called
palacinky here, but what's the diff?
Then, had to get home to meet the kids and the damn
trams
weren't running. You'd think that with 1,000 years of
history, they'd be able to figure out how to run a
tram in the snow, wouldn't you? Nah. Had to hail a
taxi, negotiate (in Czech, which is interesting since
I can barely eke out a coherent sentence) and skid and
wiggle home. The car was sliding all over the road,
too...
Hope yer well.
CW
```

Our last couple of days in Lanzarote were spent sight-seeing and enjoying the beaches, and when it came time to fly home, we wished we could stay for another week. After a five hour flight back to Prague, we landed at Ruzyne Airport, and I couldn't help recall landing there in August. We had been utterly bewildered. But now we really knew our way around. I used my Czech phone card to call a taxi from AAA, and within an hour of landing, we were on our way home. As the taxi wended through the now-familiar streets, I recalled how strange the buildings, cars, and stores had looked in the beginning. Now they were all familiar and comforting.

After lugging our suitcases up the three flights of stairs to our apartment, we kicked off our shoes and opened the door.

"It feels good to be home," Stephanie said.

Keeping Connected

Everyone in the family, especially Stephanie and I, used e-mail extensively in order to keep up with friends. My mother wrote us letters and faithfully called every Sunday. We sent lots of postcards. But our dog, Sherlock, was completely out of touch, and I missed him terribly. We had left him at the home of the local vet, and on a few occasions we called to check in on him. The conversations went pretty much like this: "How's Sherlock?" "Oh, he's fine." They couldn't tell if Sherlock missed us, and Sherlock didn't have the decency to bark in the background or howl plaintively, so we gave up calling. However, though it's pretty useless to call the dog, having a cheap phone service is essential.

Both of our apartments came equipped with operating telephones—a must in a country where touchtone dialing is still being introduced. But international rates using the Czech system are outrageously high, so I set up a "callback account" for phoning the U.S. It cost only about 30 cents per minute—compared to the $4 to $5 per minute I would have paid using the domestic phone system or my AT&T calling card.

To use a callback system, you dial a U.S. "trigger number," let it ring once, then hang up. A few seconds later, the system's computer calls you back. Voice prompts walk you through the steps of placing a call to anywhere in the world.

Callback systems require tone dialing—the little beeps you hear when you press the keypad buttons. Even if a phone has a keypad, it may not have tone dialing. Some phones can be switched from pulse to tone; that's what we used. If your phone uses pulse dialing only, small keypads that attach to the mouthpiece and transmit the tones are available from the callback service and from stores such as Radio Shack.

Callback systems are offered by several companies who usually charge a small monthly fee. All phone charges, plus the fee, are charged to your credit card so that record keeping is easy.

Banking on It

Moving out of the country for a year, our goal was to stuff as much financial information as possible onto the computer for better organization.

We signed up for on-line banking, which at our bank in California was free of charge. With 8,000 miles between us and the friendly tellers at the local branch back in Ojai, we could use the service to transfer money between accounts and—though we didn't use the system—to pay bills.

Setting up on-line banking takes only a few minutes. You can probably get a setup disk at your local branch or by calling the bank's 800 number or logging on to its Web site for instructions.

With a single bank's site, however, you're limited to transactions involving that bank. For greater flexibility, use a financial management program, such as Quicken or Microsoft Money. With these, you can download credit card transactions, pay and sometimes receive bills, and transfer money between accounts that are at the same institution.

Other Measures

Your objective should be to streamline your financial system and make your life back home operate as automatically as possible. Consider setting up automatic deposits for regularly occurring income, and automatic withdrawals for recurring expenses such as the home mortgage, auto payments, or life insurance. Setting up impound accounts for property taxes and homeowner's insurance[7]—though it might cost something in lost interest income—is one way to ensure that these funds are available when needed.

Plan "B" from Outer Space

At the time we lived abroad—1997 to 1998—Quicken didn't yet offer international Internet-based on-line bill payment, and our bank's system was unwieldy. We had our accountant listed as a signer on our checking account, and she paid those bills that were not paid by automatic deduction and sent us monthly statements. Even if you've set up everything to run automatically, consider making such an arrangement with a trusted person back home—ideally your accountant, financial adviser, or attorney—in case of an emergency.

---

[7]Usually, mortgage companies will collect the funds for property taxes and homeowner's insurance, then disburse the funds when due.

A Cash Economy

In Prague, credit cards are widely accepted, but as in much of the world, cash is the preferred medium of payment, especially for person-to-person transactions. Europeans—including our landlord—just don't grasp the idea of the personal check. "Yes, it just looks like a printed slip of paper, but I sign my name on it and it's *as good as real money.*"

We tried to pay cash for everything. It required a lot more record keeping, and I'd always have a pocket full of receipts at the end of the day, but it helped us keep our spending under control. However, you will need, and want, a credit card, too. Get one from an American institution, because the rates and terms of payment are far more reasonable.

Electronic Transfers

Despite its roots in American soil, ISP banked with a German bank and discouraged personal checks by attaching a $50 processing fee to each check. The favored method of payment there, as is often the case for large transactions, is the electronic funds transfer between banks. If you're not familiar with how these work, ask your bank for the appropriate forms prior to departure, and make sure that whoever is overseeing your finances back home is familiar with the procedure.

EIGHT

A Night at
(what we thought was)
the Opera

"You know you're an expat when... your kids are on the phone making international calls to their friends."

—David Howard, Spain

When you're a freelance expatriate, you're there by choice, even when you're going through culture shock and wonder why you're there at all. Whatever happens, you have the comfort, or the misery, of knowing that you chose it.

Corporate and embassy personnel don't have that same freedom. In December, Kelsey was invited to a classmate's birthday party. The family had rented a small movie theater for a showing of *The Hunchback of Notre Dame*. In the lobby, I met the father, who was Dutch, and when I told him I was impressed that he and his wife had invited the whole class, he said he thought it was important for his daughter. "She may never see many of them again." he said. "We'll be leaving at the end of the month." His company had transferred him to Paraguay.

For a while I felt sorry for the guy, being yanked around the globe like that. Then I realized how much he was probably making and I didn't feel so bad.

Subject: (no subject)
Date: Mon, 09 Feb 1998 08:14:25 +0100
From: Chris Westphal
To: Terry Harris

Terry,
I'd like to get some copies of *Echo Valley*. How??
-crw

Subject: Re: (no subject)
Date: Tue, 10 Feb 1998 11:19:55 EST
From: Terry Harris
To: Chris Westphal

Dear Chris,
Thanks for the e-mail. Things are sorting themselves
out slowly here now; I am sorry not to have been able
to keep you properly informed. Bruno Janlois and I now
have the framework to publish a modest list here in
the UK and to continue to publish a goodly proportion
of American writers. We hope to be able to re-open
offices in NYC in due course but cannot put a date on
that as yet. We are publishing with the imprint
Worcestershire Publishing, as fortunately the other
partner had no shares of financial connections with
this company so it is 'clean.' Cynthia Kear is re-
signing with Worcestershire and we have signed on a
few more writers of both fiction and non-fiction. Its
been a slog and the next 6 months will not be easy,
but at least we are still in business and are able to
continue with our policies.
I have some stock of *Echo Valley*; how many copies do
you require and where should they be sent?
Regards,
Terry

But the life of the career expatriate is usually a transient one.
While those we met were open, generous, and friendly, they under-
standably kept a certain distance. One day, the mother of one of
Drew's ISP friends said to Stephanie, "Tell me how long you're going
to stay so I'll know how much to like you." It wasn't said in a cold-
hearted way at all, but rather out of vulnerability. She had made—

and lost—many friends and didn't want to invite such loss again.

Not being career expats, we often felt out of place among the corporate and diplomatic families with children at ISP. We didn't have a lot of the perks they had, but we did have freedom.

We also felt a little out of place with Stephanie's teacher friends, but for entirely different reasons. Of the 100 or so teachers working for the Caledonian, she was the only one who had her family with her. Most of the other teachers were in their twenties, with a few in their fifties and sixties. Virtually all of them were single and had a lot fewer obligations than we did. But within both groups, we found common ground with many people.

By February, we were firmly ensconced in the two disparate worlds: English teachers there on a lark, and career expatriates. We formed a writing group with some of Stephanie's colleagues. Thanks to invitations from Eva, who works with the Austrian Cultural Institute, we saw wonderful music and choral performances by visiting artists. On weekends, we toured castles, museums, and ancient cities. Family life was taking on a new intimacy. Because we had all done so many new things together, there was always something to talk about, something to wonder about.

Now, after six months of living in Prague, all of our lives were full of activities and interesting friends. Two of these new friends were Jeff Lyons, a gifted cartoonist, and his fiancé, Mary Salmena. Mary taught English at the Caledonian, while Jeff was using his time abroad to work on illustrating various projects for children in hopes of finding a publisher. They were from Canada, and though they were

TIP: When purchasing air tickets, use a credit card that provides insurance coverage in case of accident, as well as other protections.

MORE DATA, PLEASE...
American Medical Centers operates medical centers in Eastern Europe that offer western style medical care. Their Web site also offers a variety of links to other travel health-related sites. Visit them at www.amcenters.com. American Medical Centers Management Co., Inc., 143 Newbury Street, 6th Floor, Boston, MA 02116-2925, Tel: (from US or Canada) 877.952.6262, Tel: (from all other locations): +1.617.262.5301, fax: +1.617.262.5302, E-mail: headquarters@amcenters.com

Expat Answers:
"Think carefully about moving to a new country if you have a condition that requires regular medical supervision or trips to an emergency room, like severe allergies or diabetes, heart conditions, digestive disorders, etc. Stress lowers resistance, and a big change, such as moving to a new country, results in more stress."
–Peggy Krikava, Prague

TIP: When possible, bring the pill form or powdered form of medications instead of the liquid variety. The medication will stay fresh for a longer period of time, and there is, of course, no risk of a spill.

much younger than we were—Mary was in her late twenties; Jeff had just turned 30—we had a lot in common with them. Jeff looked to me for advice on how to approach publishers. Mary and Stephanie, both teaching, could commiserate. Best of all, Jeff and Mary had terrific senses of humor. Like us, they had come to Prague as something of a lark, so we were able to also share with them the emotional ups and downs of expatriate life. Since their arrival, they'd become devotees of opera, of which there are many in Prague. In February, they asked if we'd join them for a performance of *Carmen*.

I'm the resident lowbrow, so I said, "Oh, I'm really not much of an opera fan."

"Neither was I," said Jeff. "But these are great—even if you can't understand the language."

Stephanie does enjoy opera, and I thought that if Jeff could rise to the occasion, so could I. We agreed to go.

"You won't be disappointed," Jeff assured us.

A Tale of TVs, Midgets, and Dancing Nazis

A few days before the performance, Stephanie and I took the tram down to the theater, where we presented our residency permits, and for a trifling 40 crowns each—about $1.10—we bought our tickets.

Entering the sumptuous National Theater—a central point of Czech culture and pride—we found our seats high up in the balcony. For 40 crowns, you can't expect to sit next to the orchestra pit. No problem. There was no orchestra anyway. But as I looked down at the set, I realized other strange things. The stage looked like a frat house after a party. Clothes were strewn about, and large television monitors were arrayed along either side.

"Uh-oh," said Jeff.

The lights went down. The TV monitors, awash with flickering snow, came on. We settled back, now having no idea what to expect.

A midget came onstage, pushing a wheelbarrow. Methodically, he began picking up the clothing and tossing it into the barrow. A discordant dirge came from the speaker system. Then, a prison scene unfolded. To the dull thud of a droning percussion soundtrack, dancers in prison garb marched around the perimeter. Guards wearing some kind of Nazi uniform strutted around, keeping the prisoners in place.

But what about Carmen? Where was Carmen?

```
Subject: Re: Books
Date: Thu, 12 Feb 1998 08:05:40
From: Chris Westphal
To: Terry Harris

Terry,
Please send 25 copies of Echo Valley for promotional
purposes to me at:

Na Petynce 104
Prague 6 - Stresovice
169 00 Czech Republic
telephone: 420 2/ 243 14 569

I would also like your telephone number.
Thanks,
Chris Westphal
```

As the monotonous march continued, a few notes of an aria could be heard over the now screeching soundtrack. Then came something that sounded like power saws and breaking glass. Lots of breaking glass. Jeff and Mary slumped in their seats. But Stephanie and I were practically choking with laughter. This wasn't an opera at all, but an interpretive fatuous, artsy, ballet-opera-performance piece; one can imagine the creator "re-envisioning" and "modernizing" the piece for a "sophisticated" audience.

And they got us.

```
Subject: Still no books
Mon, 23 Feb 1998 16:57:03 +0100
From: Chris Westphal
To: Terry Harris

Dear Terry,
Have you sent the 25 promotional books, as requested?
Do let me know. I am going to be in London March 21,
22 & 23 at the Int'l Book Fair, and may be able to
make something happen.
Chris Westphal
```

There were pirouetting Nazis aplenty. At one point, to the accompaniment of the screeching sound track, rival gangs squared off in a knife fight right out of *West Side Story*.

Then the scene transitioned to a western saloon, where the main characters—Carmen may have been a saloon girl—played poker. One of the players was cheating and got shot.

Later, a big dance number featured lots of scantily clad women wearing white swimming caps with a diagonal red stripe across the top; they looked like international exit signs. Not once, but several times, the dancers did gymnastic, erotic dances—or, more precisely, poses— with a set of black, high-backed, three-legged chairs. We still hadn't identified Carmen.

When a balding dancer came out, Stephanie whispered, "There's something so appealing about a dancer with long, thin, stringy hair."

"Maybe that's Carmen!" I suggested.

Then, the scene suddenly shifted back to the prison. Maybe the saloon had been a flashback, or maybe it was from an entirely separate production. The dancing Nazis were still trying to get the prisoners under control, this time by spinning and kicking at them.

Stephanie whispered to me, "You get back in your cell, or I'll pirouette really close!"

"These toe shoes are registered as lethal weapons!" I added.

```
Subject: Any info? (Part 1)
Date: Tue, 24 Feb 1998 09:50:55 +0100
From: Chris Westphal
To: Cynthia Kear
```

Hi,
Do you have any somewhat up-to-date contact information
on our elusive publisher? He has fallen silent again
(I guess it's hard to use a keyboard when you're in a
straight-jacket). I find it more than bizarre that he
talks about buying new manuscripts when he seems to
make no effort whatsoever to sell the books he's
already published! I'm going to London to the
International Book Fair—something any competent publisher would do when it's an event an hour's drive
from his supposed office—and I can't even get this
bozo to answer a yes or no question.
Aaaayyyyyyyahhhhaaaaaaahhhhhhhh!!!!
Chris Westphal

Various brawls ensued, and in the end, almost everyone was dead—even Carmen, I think, though who she actually was remained unclear. Finally, the stringy-haired dancer remained onstage alone, sweating under a spotlight. The midget from the opening scene reappeared from the wings, solemnly cradling a bleached cow's skull under his arm, and proceeded to move some of the sets off-stage.

The lone dancer stood mournfully in the middle of the stage while discordant music and the sounds of crashing glass set our teeth on edge.

Finally, the dancer pivoted, then marched to the rear of the stage and went through a heavy prison door. A resounding SLAM echoed across the stage. The lights were doused.

"Oh my God!" Jeff blurted out with perfect timing. Half the theater erupted in laughter.

Outside the theater, Jeff said, "Well, sorry about that. The others have been so good."

"Oh, I thought it was great," I said. "One of the funniest things I've ever seen. I'll have to go to the opera more often."

```
Subject: Re: Any info? (Part 2)
Date: Wed, 25 Feb 1998 09:37:34
From: Chris Westphal
To: Cynthia Kear
```

Herr Terry is still underground. I did contact (via the
Web) some British publisher's association, and they
gave me his correct address, etc., along with the same
telephone number that never answers. So, in some
respects he DOES exist in the official establishment.
I'll only be in England for 2 1/2 days, so unfortunately won't have a chance to train up to Worcestershire
unless the fair is just a crashing failure, in which
case I'll ditch it and make my way up to Terry's mythi-
cal Well's House... which is probably some dilapidated
council flat in the middle of the slums. Terry's out
front playing 3-card Monty with his Pakistani sidekick.
It all has the makings of comedy, or of murder... I
vacillate between the two. But don't get me started.
Later,
Chris

Weaving a Safety Net

When Kelsey came down with croup while in Prague, we knew the drill: fire up the shower and stand with her in the billowing steam, then bundle her up and take her out into the frigid night air. When she's breathing a little easier, dose her with the codeine-based cough medicine we'd brought along. If it got really bad, we had brought along enough abuterol inhalers to stock an asthma asylum.

We had purchased a health insurance policy underwritten by Reliance that would kick in after a small deductible. Coverage cost about $2,500 per year for our family of four—half of the cost of our domestic insurance—and provided $250,000 in coverage. It's vital that any insurance policy includes provisions for repatriation and emergency evacuation. Before leaving, I'd spoken to a friend who, as a reporter, had had appendicitis while on assignment at a Russian Black Sea resort. He ended up in a hospital so short of supplies that they were re-using hypodermic needles. He was helicoptered to Germany for emergency treatment.

Some domestic health insurance policies, such as Blue Cross, will cover you while overseas on vacation, but check with your insurance broker on whether the policy will still be valid, and provide the necessary benefits in the case of a long-term stay.

Admit One

Initially, we had no idea what state the Czech medical system was in. While there, though, I got freelance work editing the sometimes-bizarre translations of Czech and Slovak healthcare system newsletters. In brief, the system is a mess, not due to inadequate training or standards, but for financial and managerial reasons. The meltdown of communism as well as corruption struck hard at the medical establishment, and at the time we were there, a physician earned only about $300 per month. No wonder they were so accommodating when it came to house calls—we paid $45 cash for the convenience.

Insurance: An Exciting Topic in Any Language

While health insurance is the most important thing to consider, revising homeowner's insurance to reflect status as a rental property is also important. If you are renting your property, contact your insurer and convert your policy from homeowner's insurance to a dwelling-fire policy. The cost will be roughly the same, but you will be protected against liability, as would the owner of any rental property. Inform your tenants that they will be responsible for purchasing renter's insurance to cover personal property.

Specialty coverages, such as those for flood, earthquake, or hurricane, should remain unchanged, since they relate to the property regardless of who resides there.

Car Culture

In Prague, we found ourselves doing all kinds of cultural things that, living in a small town, we didn't often have a chance to do. But one thing that we particularly enjoyed about living abroad, especially in an urban setting, was the ability to not depend on a car to get everywhere. I've lived in Southern California for more than 20 years and owned a car since I was 16, so driving is almost second nature to me. Still, the thought of getting behind the wheel in Prague was terrifying. The streets are narrow and crooked, the traffic is horrendous, and the police are corrupt. I'd heard dozens of stories of expatriate drivers being shaken down for no reason. For us, not owning a car was something of a point of pride, too; we were intent on living as the natives do. But as the months went by, the benefits of having a car outweighed the risks.

Still, cost was a problem. A puny rental car from one of the big companies cost $100 or more a day. Then a friend at ISP recommended a small Czech rental car company that he'd used. "They only speak Czech," he warned me, "but I managed all right." This fellow had a lisp and the worst pronunciation I'd ever heard. I figured it was worth a try.

I found the office on the third floor of a small apartment building. A woman in her mid-fifties and wearing a housedress ushered me into the entry. There, a desk, chairs, and filing cabinets comprised the worldwide headquarters. The room opened onto the kitchen where, by the smell of it, some meat and cabbage had been boiling for about a month. This was truly a mom and pop operation, and I was dealing with Mom.

Using my limited Czech, I asked if there was a car available. There was, and she brought out a contract, which she was eager to discuss in minute detail. I knew the price and the liability, but beyond that, I had no idea what she was saying. I nodded convincingly as she referred to various clauses in the contract, but for all I knew, I was pledging to carry guns into Albania.

I ultimately signed the contract, and Pop, wearing slippers, emerged from the living room. Out on the street, he led me to a seven or eight-year-old red Skoda hatchback. Seven or eight years in Skoda years is equivalent to about 20 American car years. Pop showed me where the spare tire was and warned me to check the oil frequently. It was one of the two cars in the fleet, the other one being a shinier blue sedan, which the couple probably drove when it wasn't rented.

I slid behind the wheel and pulled the flimsy door closed. Surprisingly, it drove okay. We rented the car a couple of times for trips to Regensburg, Germany, and Vienna, Austria.

Eight months into our year in Prague, I rented it on a long-term basis for $11 per day. That day, as I navigated into traffic and toward home, I felt like a new member of the bourgeoisie. At the apartment, the children wanted to look at the "new" car. They were as thrilled as if I'd just brought home a new Cadillac rather than the same old heap we'd had before.

Especially with children, having a car is almost an essential. Here are a few options to consider:

Shipping Your Car Over from the U.S.

Shipping your car may be an option, particularly if you're going to an underdeveloped country. However, depending on your destination country and the length of time you plan to stay, VAT (Value Added Taxes) may be assessed, along with other fees and taxes that could add up to thousands of dollars. If you can get your car to a port, you can use a ro/ro—roll-on/roll-off—shipper, which could be more economical than shipping your car in a container. Ro/ro ships are like big floating parking garages. Costs for shipping depend on destination and on the size of the car and range from $850 and up.

Shipping a car is worth considering, but think carefully about whether it makes economic and practical sense. Compared to most cars in Europe, for example, the typical American sedan is huge. European roads are comparatively narrow. Also, in most of the world, gasoline is often two to four times more expensive than it is in the U.S. In short, do you really need a giant gas guzzler?

If you decide to ship your car, here are a few hints:

- Contact the consulate of your destination country and get all the information you can about taxes, fees, and restrictions.

- Use a shipping agent to make sure all documentation is in order. To find a shipping agent, seek recommendations via international relocation departments of major corporations, other expatriates, and the U.S. Embassy in your destination country. Try a search on the Web, too.

- Buy Marine Insurance. The carrier or shipping line has a maximum liability of $500, so if your car ends up at the bottom of the Atlantic, you'll be out of luck because your regular auto insurance won't cover the loss.

- Make sure that you've removed everything from you car prior to shipment. Ro/ro carriers do not allow goods to be left inside the vehicle—even in the trunk. There goes the plan to send your aunt over on the cheap. Shippers are not responsible for any thing left inside—and articles left in the vehicle may present a temptation to thieves.

- Don't leave too much gas in your vehicle—just enough to get it off the ship and to a fuel stop.

Buying a Car in Your Destination Country

You may be in a position to buy a new car while abroad. Major European automakers such as Mercedes-Benz and Volvo have European delivery programs. There may be restrictions on the length of time you can keep the car in the country, however, so it's important to investigate this option carefully before deciding.

If you're planning to buy a new or used car in Europe and then bring it to the U.S., make sure it complies with U.S. emission and safety standards. Many cars that look the same on the outside don't meet U.S. standards, and modifying them can be prohibitively expensive. If you don't plan to bring the car to the U.S., be prepared for the hassle of selling it in your destination country, which may not be a task you want to spend your time on while you're also trying to get back home.

Long-Term Rental

Most rental companies have long-term plans that are considerably cheaper than their daily or weekly rates. Long-term rental is an attractive option if you don't know how long you'll be staying, if you don't really need a car every day, or if you plan to travel a lot.

On a day-to-day basis, rental may be slightly more expensive, but overall it's often the most economical option—especially if you're away for weeks or months vacationing or on business. Just turn the car in and don't worry about it.

Having a car, of course, gives you a lot of freedom, but that freedom isn't total. Sometimes, the rental companies restrict countries you can take the rental car into. For example, cars rented in Germany can't be taken to the Czech Republic or to some other former Soviet bloc countries because the rates of theft are tremendous. We were restricted from taking our Czech rental car to Poland and Hungary. If you do rent a car on a long-term basis, make sure you know the restrictions and plan accordingly. If your car is stolen in a country where you weren't supposed to take it, you will, as Ricky told Lucy in *I Love Lucy,* "Have a lot of 'splainin' to do," and you may be financially liable for the entire cost.

You don't even have to worry about maintenance when you rent a car. Another advantage of long-term rental is that you can get "free" insurance by putting the charge on your credit card. Check with your credit card company and your insurer, however. Some credit cards limit liability coverage for rental cars to 30 consecutive days. One way to get around this is to charge one month on one credit card, then switch credit cards every 30 days.

NINE

A Giraffe at the Window

"You know you're an expat when...someone asks you where you are from and you don't know how to answer."

—Caryn Bunshaft, Japan

When I was 20, I took a trip to Kenya with my university. The African Studies credit I received was secondary to the chance I'd have to have an adventure in a far off and exotic land. Most of the time we were with the group, learning about subjects ranging from modern political history to anthropology to geology, but at one point two new friends and I went off together, hitchhiking from the far northern part of the country through the Great Rift Valley to Nairobi, where we stopped long enough to have dinner and a Tusker lager. Then we hit the road again, on our way to Mombassa on the coast. Our first ride dropped us on the main highway outside the city limits, and as night fell, there we stood. I had never felt further from home in my life.

After waiting for an hour or so by the side of the road, an oil truck wheezed to a stop and the driver waved us toward him. It was already dark, and we would have taken a ride to anywhere at that point, but to our delight, he said he was going to Mombassa, so we climbed aboard. As the driver throttled the rig through its gears, we asked where he was from. He spoke only Swahili, but eventually we figured out that he was from Uganda. This was during the brutal reign of Idi Amin, and for all we knew, the driver's plan was to pull along the side of the road and butcher us.

MORE DATA, PLEASE... If you or your spouse has an office computer that will remain operating in your absence, a product from ExpertCity.com, called GoToMyPC, allows you use a remote computer to operate software or obtain files from the computer in your office. Look on the Web at www.expertcity.com.

TIP: Since Windows-type PCs dominate the world market, think carefully before bringing an Apple computer with you as your sole computer. Obtaining software and service may be a problem.

But he had no such plan, though he did ask for a couple of shillings, which we gladly gave him. As we sped along the narrow highway, we tried to make conversation, but got only far enough to learn that he felt pretty lucky to have a job that got him out of Uganda, and that the only way he could stay awake was by chewing pinches of dried leaves, which were a stimulant about as strong as a stiff cup of coffee.

As the rig roared through the African night, my companions and I looked at each other, wide-eyed with wonder. Here we were in Africa! In a big rig truck! With a Ugandan driver! Even without chewing on our driver's offered leaves, we couldn't have slept through this experience. We were now no longer tourists, but adventurers. The headlights carved a path before us as we moved across the high grasses of the veldt.

Suddenly, a face appeared at the side window. Huge nostrils flared, and hairy cartoon lips curled up. "A giraffe!" someone shouted. Then, as quickly as it had come into sight, the animal was gone.

We were dazzled. "Did you see that? Incredible! A giraffe, right in the road!"

"Twiga!" we told the driver, knowing the Swahili word for the animal. He simply shrugged and waved his hand, as though to say that the encounter was nothing. Then he took another pinch of his leaves to help him through the night.

We Had Become Like that Driver

By the time March came to Prague, my family and I had become like that driver. "Giraffes" whizzed past every hour of the day and we hardly noticed. That month, we anticipated a steady stream of visitors from the

States and looked forward to showing them around town, knowing that seeing Prague through their eyes would refresh our enthusiasm. Prague was home now, and we had established not only friendships there, but also routines for daily living that made our lives seem comfortably ordinary. We felt a great sense of pride in having settled in so well.

Debra Merrill was our first visitor. Attractive and sophisticated, she is an architect from California who works as a project manager for an international development firm. We were determined to give her and her six-year-old daughter, Katy, an insider's tour not only of Prague, but also of the Czech Republic. At the time of their visit, Pastor Jim Krikava and his wife had scheduled a retreat for their church to a small pension at, as Jim described it, "the last house in the Czech Republic." It was in the small town of Jeleni, about four hours outside of Prague on the way to Germany, and we had been invited to join them both for the retreat and a mini-vacation.

Stephanie and I anticipated a weekend of skiing in the nearby Tatra Mountains, side trips to Karlovy Vary[8], and perhaps an interesting night exploring Jeleni, which we were certain no common tourist would ever visit. We eagerly invited Debra and Katy along, and they were enthusiastic. I pictured a weekend in a quaint mountain village, with icicles hanging from the eves of woodsy cabins. The town wasn't mentioned in any travel book we could find, so we were really expecting something off the beaten track.

Debra and Katy had been in the country for only a day or so when we squeezed into our tiny rented Skoda and headed out of

> **TIP:** A scanner is an essential tool for creating Web pages and comes in handy for lots of other things, including sending faxes and making photocopies. Drew and Kelsey used it regularly to insert graphics into their schoolwork. When creating Web pages, the scanner is used to scan pictures, drawings, and photos. See the manufacturer's instructions for information on its optimal use.

---

[8]In German, Karvlovy Vary is known as Carlsbad, the famous "spa" city where for centuries, European aristocrats and luminaries, including Goethe, Beethoven, Marx, Einstein, Mann, and Freud, to name a few, went to rest and recuperate. When the Czech Lands were a part of the Austro-Hungarian Empire, German was the official language, though Czech was also used.

MORE DATA, PLEASE... To find services that provide free space for Web pages, do an Internet search using keywords such as *free Web page*, *free Web site*, or *free home page*. You can also log on to www.fwpreview.com, which features reviews and links to free Web page building and hosting sites.

Prague for our mountain trip. The highway passed hops fields and wended through forests, but no matter how we tried, we could not avoid being stranded behind a diesel-spewing truck. Finally, after a long drive that had taken us through lovely pastoral scenes where old castle ruins were perched on the hilltops, as well as through bleak villages, we arrived at Jeleni.

When Jim said "the last house in the Czech Republic," he was not exaggerating. Jeleni is in the Sudatenland—ground zero of World War II, the first region conquered by the Nazis. The Nazis probably did their part to destroy it, and when the communists took over, they finished the job. Bulldozers were sent in to level every building, as Jeleni was too close to the corrupting influence of capitalist West Germany.

The pension and two smaller houses—one empty, the other abandoned—were all that was left. There would be no exploring the town, because for all practical purposes, it didn't exist. To make matters worse, there was no snow, either.

The pension, owned by a cousin of Jim's, was guarded by a decrepit, blind German shepherd dog who patrolled the downstairs lobby and snarled at everything that moved. There was a dining room with a bar downstairs, but other than that, it was simply a house that had been renovated. During snowy seasons, the pension is probably a good place for cross-country skiing and is less than a half hour away from larger alpine ski areas. But we knew we wouldn't be doing either on this trip. As the dog sniffed and snarled, we learned that Debra would be sharing a room with Stephanie and me, while Katy and the other children would share another room—not exactly five-star accommodations.

We hadn't stopped to get lunch during our drive, thinking that we could find a restaurant in Jeleni. We were left to either raid the empty house down the road or continue with the juice, stale bread, and cheese we had left over from the drive. As all the children played in another room, we pushed our suitcases aside, and on a small table along the wall, I sliced the cheese with my Swiss Army knife and passed it around. This was more like a camp out than the luxurious alpine escape we had anticipated. "Bet you're glad you came all the way from L.A. for this, aren't you?" I asked Debra, half in jest.

As we sat eating and drinking in the cramped room, we wove fanciful tales about the wonders of Jeleni and the fun we would have in this garden spot of the Czech Republic. We spent the afternoon taking a walk toward the German border, hoping that perhaps there was a bustling Bavarian village over the hill, but we saw only a forest of spindly trees on either side of the road.

That night in the pension's small dining room, we had a hearty Czech dinner of pork cutlets prepared by the affable proprietor and his wife. Unfortunately, Debra is a vegetarian—something it's very difficult to be in a country that we often referred to as "the land of the meat-eaters." She played along, though, making a dinner of the potatoes and bread served with the meal.

After dinner, Jim, who is an outstanding musician, played guitar and led sing-alongs of Czech and American songs as we drank good Czech beer and sampled some Becherovka—a potent herb liqueur made in Karlovy Vary[9]. As we joined in the songs, trying to sound out the Czech words, I realized

TIP: In Netscape Composer, your Web page will look entirely different than it will on the Web, so it's important to preview it before uploading it. To preview a page, save it and then click "Preview."

---

[9]Karlovy Vary has 12 mineral springs, each at a different temperature and with different mineral content. Depending on the ailment, doctors perscribe varying amounts of liquid to be drunk from the different springs. Becherovka was originally marketed as a medicinal treatment and is known as "the 13th spring."

TIP: The first step in creating a Web page is to create a folder on your computer desktop where all of your Web page files will go. Otherwise, the files will be spread all over your computer, and when it comes time to upload the Web page to the server, you'll be totally confused.

that it didn't really matter that things hadn't worked out for this trip as we had imagined—at least as far as our family was concerned. What was important was that we had become a part of a community. Since we had moved to the new apartment, we had been able to spend more time with the church members and with other parents at ISP.

But though she was definitely a good sport about it, I don't think Debra felt the same. We apologized repeatedly for dragging her and Katy along, and she kindly protested that she had enjoyed it. I know it was because of the people, because it couldn't have been the town.

Debra was something of a sacrifice on the part of better visitor experiences by those who followed. After that visit, we resolved to do better, and we stuck with more conventional itineraries. One component of our new plan for visitors involved Pavel Urban, a journalist who was the husband of one of Stephanie's students. Besides his excellent English and a good sense of humor, Pavel possessed an encyclopedic knowledge of Czech history and culture. For $25 or $30, he led private walking tours of the city. Typically, when visitors arrived, we arranged for Pavel to take them through the castle complex, then through the twisting streets of Old Town and into the center of the city. We would meet for lunch at Red Hot and Blues, an expat hangout.

As more visitors came in spring, we continually refined our routine. We took my mother and sister to Cesky Krumlov, a medieval city remaining virtually intact from the fourteenth century, and Telc, which dates from the Renaissance, and caught most of the major attractions in Prague. With visiting friends, we went to out-of-the-way restaurants, such as Peklo, meaning "Hell" in English, which is built into the old wine cellars of the Strahoff Monastery. We taught everyone how to navigate the city's excellent public transit system, which taxi company to use, and how to say important words like "please," "thank you," and "beer."

By June, we felt even more at ease with having guests and took more opportunities to experiment with their visits. When my brother, Roger, said that he wanted to visit with his wife and adult daughter, we were fully prepared, at least on a strategic level. Personally, it was another matter, because in 20 years, Roger has visited my home twice—and we live in the same state. I guess that living farther away had made us a lot more interesting.

Prior to their arrival, I checked out their hotel, and when their plane touched down at Prague's Ruzyne Airport, I was there with our trusty Skoda—now ours on a long-term rental contract—to pick them up. After their tour with Pavel, we delivered our standard taxi recommendations, a quick primer on use of the metro and tram system, and advised them where to find good deals on fine Czech glassware and other products.

MORE DATA, PLEASE... To download the latest version of Netscape, go to www.netscape.com and follow the links to the version of Netscape you want to download.

Playing the Palac

Living in a foreign city confers upon you a certain aura of authority, and we had come to enjoy this role. Because we generally referred visitors to Pavel for the major walking tour of the city, we were spared the more touristy activities.

As legal residents of the Czech Republic, we also got some concrete benefits, such as cheap transit passes and eligibility for steep discounts on state-subsidized theatrical performances. So it was well within our budget to treat all three of our visitors to a performance of the opera *Cosi Fan Tutti* at the baroque Estates Theater, where Mozart premiered *Don Giovanni*. This time it was a real opera, done without dwarves or televisions onstage.

On their final night in Prague, we took my brother and his family to Palffi Palac, a continental restaurant in an eighteenth-century palace in the Mala Strana area of the city. With faded white plaster walls and worn wood flooring, the restaurant exuded a charmingly faded elegance. You half expected a dissolute duke to welcome you as you entered the dimly lit rooms. We enjoyed a wonderful meal, and after dessert, the waiter asked if we'd like anything else.

"Do you have absinthe?" I asked. Absinthe is still produced in the Czech Republic, though it's illegal almost everywhere, and as a result, it is surrounded by considerable mystique. Besides being made at least partially of wood alcohol derived from wormwood, it is also a throat-searing 140 proof, or 70 percent alcohol. Allegedly, it drives you insane, too, which probably made its popularity among early twentieth century writers and artists all the more scandalous. It was okay for writers and artists to cook their brains in the stuff, but legend has it that a French farmer murdered his family under the influence of absinthe, and consequently it was made illegal. It has remained so ever since and has accumulated over the years a rather sinister reputation. Of course, we had to try it.

Everyone ordered a glass, and we were puzzled when the waiter brought not only small aperitif glasses full of a faint emerald green liquid, but also a sugar dispenser, some spoons, and a packet of matches.

"What do we do with all this?"

"Oh, you've never tried?"

"Uh, no."

"I'll show you." The waiter filled a spoon with absinthe, then poured in perhaps a quarter teaspoon of sugar. "You light," he said.

I put a match to the liquid and it burned with a clear blue flame. After a minute or so, the sugar had melted. The waiter dribbled the resulting liquid into my glass of absinthe. "Now you drink." It tasted somewhat like black licorice, but it burned so much as it went down that taste was rather secondary.

We took turns firing up each other's teaspoons-full of absinthe. Since we had already had drinks before dinner and a bottle or two of wine with dinner, the joke that "absinthe makes the heart grow fonder" seemed wildly funny. Besides that, the ritualistic method of consumption made the whole episode seem more than a bit illicit.

When it was Roger's turn, he grew momentarily hypnotized with the flickering blue flame on his spoon. Before it went out, he started dumping the spoon's flaming contents into his glass. When the liquid in his glass caught fire, he panicked, spilling what was left in the spoon onto the table. Glass, table, and spoon were now burning. Fortunately, he managed to suffocate the flames with his napkin, so we were all howling with laughter instead of howling with pain or getting hauled off to the nearest burn ward. The waiter looked on, amused at our incompetence.

Enjoying this exotic ceremony in this wonderful and quirky locale, we were part of this place. My brother and his wife were visiting Prague, but they were also visiting the people we had become in Prague. Against the backdrop of the city, and owing to our experiences, we had become interesting people, possessing arcane knowledge, facts, and alliances. Especially while enjoying visits from family and friends, we were no longer the apathetic, uninterested driver of that oil truck pushing through the African night. We were the giraffe. While visitors passed by, we were caught in their high beams, and we in turn glimpsed our surroundings afresh, however briefly. As they roared off in a cloud of exhaust, we continued loping across the plain.

Stepping into the Web

Because of their versatility, computers are sometimes referred to as universal machines; if you can think of a task, there's probably a way that a computer can make it easier. If you're planning to live overseas and you're not computer literate now—especially in terms of Internet use—there could be no better investment of your time than to learn how to use one. As discussed earlier, we used our computers on a daily basis for banking, e-mailing, and faxing, but they also did service in entertainment. In our quest to pare down our luggage, we brought computer versions of Monopoly and Risk, and while we were in Prague, we bought a number of other computer games.

Another excellent use for the computer is as an aid to learning the language. Instructional CD-ROMs and DVDs are available in many languages, and they make language learning more interactive than ordinary audio tapes. If you or your child is a musician, you can either bring along the actual Steinway or a computerized piano-type keyboard.

Finding an Internet Service Provider

If you have an account with America On-line, Earthlink, or even some of the smaller Internet Service Providers (ISPs), you may be able to simply get a local access number prior to your departure and keep your existing account. Since I had a small, locally-based ISP at home, this option wasn't available to me, so I had to find an ISP on my own. Months before leaving, I did an Internet search and found several service providers in Prague. I then e-mailed them, but I wasn't able to set up an account ahead of time—first, because they didn't accept credit cards, and less importantly, because I didn't know exactly where we'd be. I didn't want to be in an area of the city that, for whatever reason, they didn't serve.

Within days of arriving in Prague, I found the offices of Terminal.cz, one of the ISPs I had contacted, and paid cash to open an account with them. Since Terminal is a small organization, they gave me a lot of help in setting up the service. They even offered to come to our apartment for a small fee and set up the computers themselves. My major obstacle was that the dial tone in the Czech Republic is different than the one in the U.S. As a result, my modem didn't recognize it and refused to dial. In the modem setup, I simply told the modem not to wait for a tone, but to just dial, and that worked fine.

One thing to be aware of is that local calls are not necessarily free as they are in the U.S. In the Czech Republic, what we would refer to as "local" calls cost a couple of cents per minute. It still didn't stop me from checking e-mail several times an hour, though.

Cyber Family Westphal

I loved getting and sending e-mail, but for me, one of the most enjoyable uses of the computer was setting up a family Web site. Our Web site, with a blazing fluorescent green banner that said "Cyber Family Westphal," featured photos and text about Prague and environs, my résumé, links to friends' pages, plus photos of the children and information about them. I wanted friends—especially the children's classmates—to be able to take a look at it and get some feel for where we were and what we were doing. I was amazed from time to time to get an e-mail from a stranger who had seen my site; so if you make a Web site, be careful about posting sensitive information.

Masters of Your Domain (Name)

Before you protest that Web sites are for techno-nerds, log on to Bigstep.com at www.bigstep.com. There, following simple step-by-step directions, you can create a Web page for your family in a matter of a few minutes. And it's all free.

With Bigstep, you can actually run a Web-based business, including a catalog and shopping cart, for nothing. While abroad, you might be able to operate a home-based business or provide some type of service on-line.

Only if you use Bigstep's "premium" services or accept credit cards on your site do you pay a fee. Your Web address will be www.mywebpage.big-step.com, so it doesn't have the panache of a "dotcom" address, but at this writing—in the midst of a major shakeout among dotcom businesses—that isn't much of a sacrifice. The only downside is that when people go to your home page, a narrow Bigstep banner will display at the top of the screen.

If you already own a Web domain name, you can transfer it to Bigstep for a one-time $15 fee. You can still use Bigstep's Web page creation tools and park your site on their servers.

Basic Web Site Glossary

Domain Name: A Web site ending in one of a number of extensions, such as .com, .net, .tv. Outside the U.S., .co.uk is the United Kingdom's equivalent of .com. It costs about $35 per year to register a domain name using services such as networksolutions.com, register.com, or others.

Download: Retrieving files from the Internet.

File: Any text or graphic that is carried on your Web site.

FTP: File Transfer Protocol; the software application that records your Web page onto the Server.

Graphic: Any visual element on a Web page, for example, a photograph, logo, or other image.

Home page: The first page of your Web site. In Web-speak, this is also sometimes referred to as the Index page.

Host: The company that has your Web site on its server.

HTML: HyperText Markup Language. The "code" in which Web pages are written. If you're ever looking at a Web page, just click View, Page Source, and you'll see the HTML code that is operating in the background of most Web sites. *You don't need to know HTML to create a Web page!*

Index: The home page of your Web site, usually featuring some text, a picture or two and links to other pages of the Web site.

ISP: Internet Service Provider.

Link: A highlighted area of text that takes your browser to another Web page or file on your site. For example, a link might take you to a photograph on your site. When you're creating a Web page, you also "link" graphics to the page where they will appear on your Web site. Links can also take you to an entirely different Web site.

Server: The computer on which your Web site resides.

Upload: Sending files to the server.

Web page: One "page" of a Web site, for example, a photograph and text about a recent excursion.

Going Solo

If you're a bit more technically sophisticated, you might want to try the next level in creating a Web page and tackle the job using other tools. The advantage is greater design flexibility. You'll need to find a server, but that's simple. Typically, Internet Service Providers will give you space for a Web page when you sign up for their service.

Then, you can select from a wide array of applications to create and upload your Web page. Using Netscape, I created my own Web page in Prague, which is a pretty clear indication that it's fairly easy.

After you've found out whether your ISP will host a page, you'll need a program to compose the Web page. Fortunately, Netscape Navigator 4.7x includes Netscape Composer, which is a simple WYSIWYG (What You See Is What You Get) Web page creation tool. Microsoft Explorer's equivalent application is called Front Page and is a part of the Microsoft Office suite.

To use Netscape Composer, just open Netscape and choose Communicator, Composer. Enter text as you would in any word processing program, or import text files from elsewhere. Using "Insert an Image," you can import images in the same manner that they are imported in word processing programs such as Microsoft Word.

Links are one of the most important elements of any Web page. Whenever you see highlighted text—usually blue—in a Web page, that's a link to an image, Web page, or Web site. For example, you might have a link that says "See My Résumé." When a viewer clicks on that link, he or she will be taken to another Web page featuring your résumé.

To create such a link in Netscape Composer, first create a Web version of your resume and save it. In Microsoft Word, for example, you can use "File, Save as...," and select "Web page" in the "Save as..." dialog box. In Composer, choose "Insert, Link." In the text box under the heading "Link, Source," enter "See My Résumé." Then, click "Choose File" to select the resume Web page you've already created.

Once you've created your Web site, you need to upload it to the host, or server, where it will reside. Netscape Composer comes with an FTP application that's easy to use, but before uploading your new Web page, you'll need to find out the exact file name to use. Generally, it will be something like www.ispname/public/~yourname/pagename.htm.

If you can't get this information from your ISP, Netscape Composer has comprehensive help files that will walk you through the process.

Once you've gotten the information you need, just open your home or index page in Netscape Composer and click "Publish." Fill out the dialog box that appears as follows:

Page Title: Enter the name of the Web page.

HTML Filename: Enter the file name of your index, for example, c:/windows/desktop/mywebpage/index.htm.

HTTP or FTP Location to Publish to: Enter the location provided by your ISP, probably something like www.yourisp/public. Make sure you enter this file name precisely.

User Name: The user name you have with your ISP.

Password: The password you have with your ISP.

Other Files to Include: Choose "Files associated with this page."

With the "Publish" dialog box still open, go on-line with your ISP and click OK. The index file and any other html files you created that are linked to it will upload to the server. You can then use your browser to view your site on the World Wide Web.

The amount of time you spend creating and updating a Web site can range from a few hours a month to a several hours a day, but it's a great way not only to keep family and friends conscious of your existence, but also to keep a continuing record of your experiences for your own enjoyment.

However much time you spend building and upgrading your Web site, the activity can be a great creative outlet when the isolation of being abroad starts to feel oppressive.

TEN

Defying Gravity

"You know you're an expat when... you get excited seeing commercials on the TV shows your family taped for you."

-Vanessa Sobotta, Japan

Moving abroad is something like going into space. Breaking the bonds with earth takes tremendous energy, both mentally and physically, as does leaving your home country. Then once the bond is broken, you suddenly become weightless and disoriented. Even ordinary things are remarkable. But after a while, weightlessness becomes the norm, and gravity seems odd.

After nine months in Prague, we'd adjusted to life outside the gravitational pull of the United States. Standing in line at the post office to pay the phone bill didn't seem odd to me anymore. Presenting our tram passes to the undercover transit police was a matter of routine. We didn't think about how things were done in the States because it really didn't matter. We were here, not there, and we had grown to accept that things were just different.

Over the previous nine months, Stephanie and I had endured several cycles of culture shock, ranging from disillusionment to enchantment, and lots in between. Prague had virtually become a third party to our marriage. In the winter, while I felt bleak and dispirited because of Terry Harris' elusiveness and unreliability about publishing my book, Stephanie was in high gear. She loved urban life and enjoyed teaching, particularly when a class would consist of sitting in one of Prague's many atmospheric cafes and discussing the news of the day with a student. Prague was serenading her with a song about city life that made the melodies of our life back home seem like a dirge.

Drew and Kelsey were both excelling in school and, thanks to our more convenient location, were able to participate fully in the activities the school had to offer. Their wide circle of friends as well as their quick acceptance and popularity had made adjustment to life abroad relatively easy for them. Drew especially enjoyed a measure of freedom that he had never known before—we let him take the taxi to and from Aaron's house. This would have been unthinkable before we left. Let our 10-year-old son get into a taxi alone? Never! However, we had discovered AAA Taxi in Prague, which was always reliable and reasonable. Calling a taxi and having them pick you up gives you a measure of protection that you don't have if you hail a taxi on the street, because the dispatcher has a record of the fare. We still insisted that Drew call us once he arrived at Aaron's, and that he also let us know when he was headed home.

By the beginning of the year, it had became undeniably clear to me that Terry Harris was either a dreamer or a mental case, so I pressed ahead with trying to find a European publisher for Echo Valley on my own. Through a former literary agent of mine in the U.S., I contacted a prominent Geneva-based agent who specialized in selling European rights. She was eager to take on Echo Valley, so that meant she would cover the major European countries—Germany, Italy, France, and the Netherlands—while Kristen Olsen would handle the Czech Republic.

Having already had the experience that agents can only do so much, I made plans in March to visit London to attend the International Book Fair, where I would pursue finding a publisher on my own, too. Before going, I sent an e-mail to Terry Harris, who surprised me not only by answering, but by agreeing to meet me in Oxford during my stay. When we met there, he said, he would finally explain his long and mysterious silences.

The book fair was a huge publishing event, and I spent hours trolling the visitors' area, scanning name badges. Whenever I'd spot an editor, publisher, or even an agent, (you can never have too many) I'd make my pitch about Echo Valley and was successful in getting half a dozen editors to take a look at the book. For an unknown author, I considered this networking a success.

Terry Harris Explains It All

On Sunday, I took the train to Oxford and waited for Terry Harris in the rundown cafe at the station, drinking watery coffee and fully expecting him to stand me up. But to my great surprise, he did appear, looking haggard and pale.

He'd looked haggard and pale when I'd met him a year earlier in New York, but this time there was a certain look of defeat in his eyes. He sat across from me and didn't order anything. We exchanged pleasantries—though I felt nothing pleasant toward him. Then he proceeded to tell me a convoluted tale of having been betrayed by his business partners while he was in New York working diligently, of course, to market *Echo Valley*. In his absence, his British partner had absconded with the business, he said, forcing him to return to England to figure out the situation. But he returned too late. Though Terry assured me that *Echo Valley* had sold out its initial printing of 3,000, Roberts had taken all the money that it made. Conveniently, for Terry at least, Roberts had also taken the sales records and documentation. Terry was left with nothing, and I was left with nothing.

Despite the fact that royalties on those sales would have amounted to several thousand dollars, I couldn't help but feel sorry for Terry as he told me he had no idea what he would do next.

But Terry Harris was the type of person who always had a back-up plan.

```
Subject: Relaunch of Echo
Date: Wed, 6 May 1998 12:30:02
From: Terry Harris
To: Chris Westphal

Dear Chris,
I am now in a position to carry on from where I left
off, so to speak, which is to launch a series of First
Novels both here in the UK and in the United States.
Naturally I would love to have you back on board and
include Echo in this. In order to do so I will have to
print a fresh edition, as this will all take place
with Worcestershire Publishing. It is my intention to
move to the West Coast and set up offices there, prob-
ably in SF.
I do know you were looking for an alternate publisher
and of course you may well be fixed up with someone
else by now. If not and if you would like to be part
```

```
of this bandwagon, please let me know.
Many thanks, It took a little time to regroup but
First Novels are back, and this time they are here to
stay.
Best,
Terry
```

Needless to say, I read of Terry Harris' new and ambitious plan with a certain level of distrust. Still, with or without him, I was feeling upbeat about my prospects of finding a European publisher. As spring arrived, I saw an attendant improvement in my mood. Perhaps this was because it is almost impossible to be in a bad mood in Prague in spring. On the tree-lined streets, fresh green leaves contrasted with the red tile roofs. The grassy parks burst into bloom. Everyone seemed to smile more.

Actually, it was Stephanie who noted how the leaves contrasted with the rooftops and that the flowers in the parks were blooming. All right, she noticed the smiles, too. I was more impressed with the women. Tall and statuesque, Czech women are classically beautiful, having heart-shaped faces and high cheekbones. But in winter, the beautiful ones apparently get shipped out, replaced with squat, dowdy surrogates wearing long mink coats and heavy boots.

With the arrival of spring, the scowling, frumpy women get rounded up and replaced with gorgeous supermodels wearing micro-miniskirts and tall platform shoes. Strolling on Vaclavske Namesti was like walking on a fashion show runway in Paris. Beautiful girls, charmingly unaware of their beauty, paraded along the sidewalks, their long silken hair blowing behind them.

This environment can be hazardous to married men, especially when they're with their wives. I spent a lot of time looking at my shoes.

```
Subject: Re: Relaunch of Echo
Date: Wed, 13 May 1998 09:42:47
From: Chris Westphal
To: Terry Harris

Dear Terry,
Interesting news. Please send me a contract—either by
post or attached file, along with any other specific
information you have—and I'll give you an answer as
soon as possible.
Regards,
Chris Westphal
```

Besides girl watching—not exactly a family sport—travel seemed like a good idea that spring. Friends at ISP had raved about Budapest, so I hastily arranged a four-day stay, mostly via the Internet. We'd gotten recommendations of restaurants and sights to see and, most importantly, the names of reputable taxi companies.

Unfortunately, the hotel that most people recommended, the opulent Gellert (Hungarian for "out of your budget") was out of our budget. But I thought I'd hit the jackpot when on the Web I found a "luxury, executive apartment" for only about $90 per night. Yes, I reasoned, we'd have to scramble our own eggs for breakfast, but as it was an "executive" residence, maybe the place offered some other amenities: a spa, a big-screen TV, or a balcony affording a splendid view of the city.

On the last day of April, we boarded a first class train and headed across the beautiful Czech countryside toward Hungary.

It was near midnight when the train rolled into Budapest's Keleti Station. Like a lot of buildings in Budapest, the station was under renovation, meaning it looked as though it had just sustained a prolonged air raid. Dodging the rubble on the ground, Kelsey—barely awake—dragged her wheeled suitcases behind her. Drew, normally gregarious and energetic, clung to Stephanie.

```
Subject: Re: Relaunch of Echo
Date: Wed, 13 May 1998 14:28:04
From: Terry Harris
To: Chris Westphal

Dear Chris,
Much will depend on if you still want to run with me.
I am pretty far along with launch plans for LA and SF.
I do not want to spend time preparing a contract until
I know if you want one or not and the date when you
return to the USA.
Please let me know.
Thanks,
Terry
```

The Executive Dungeon

As soon as we emerged from the dilapidated station and into a cold drizzle, a mob of chattering taxi drivers surrounded us. We'd gotten used to the laconic Prague taxi drivers, who'd usually prefer to smoke and talk rather than take a fare, so we were a little taken aback by this scene.

It was like being at a bazaar in downtown Iraq, and we were the merchandise. "Taxi here!" "Here! My taxi!" "Where you go?"

I held out a slip of paper on which I had written our reservation information. Animatedly, the drivers discussed the destination among themselves.

"Three thousand!" one of them offered me.

Drew grabbed my leg. "No. Don't take one of these taxis!"

"It's fine, Drew."

Dad wasn't about to be coerced into taking one of these taxis anyway, because Dad had brought with him the list of reputable taxi companies, and none of these vultures was on the list. Dad had even gotten some Hungarian currency to use at a pay phone to call a safe taxi. Unfortunately, Dad hadn't gotten any coins, and our Czech phone card wasn't valid in Hungary. In other words, Dad's plan was something other than flawless.

So while the drivers hounded us, we stood there, uncertain of what to do. Should I leave Stephanie and the children while I went into the night, searching for a shop to buy a phone card? Absolutely not. Should we all troop off together, dragging our suitcases? Nope. Is there a better way to look like a target than to wander with suitcase-toting children around dark, unfamiliar streets? I couldn't think of one.

"Twenty-five hundred!" shouted a swarthy driver with Rasputin eyes.

"No," I said. I was still contemplating my next move.

Standing in the rain and looking like confused idiots is apparently a very good tactic for getting a good fare, because soon the price for our journey was plunging.

"Twenty-two hundred!" shouted one of the drivers.

"Two thousand!" countered Rasputin.

"No." I waved a wad of forints, meaning to indicate that I needed change. "A store...?" However, waving money apparently meant, "Hey, I've got cash and I'm ready to give it to the right guy."

Rasputin bit his lip. "Fifteen hundred," he said. The other drivers walked away in disgust. This guy was badly undercutting the market.

"I said no," I told him.

With a heavy sigh, Rasputin made his final offer. "Twelve-hundred," he said.

"Okay!"

"Huh?" asked Stephanie.

"Stephanie, it's six bucks. And it's late. Let's just get out of here."

"Okay. But I hope this guy's all right."

"He's fine."

We piled into Rasputin's old Audi, and as we fumbled for our seat belts, he gunned it, swerving onto the wet street. I couldn't find my seat belt but figured, hey, he's a professional. Silly me.

A cigarette dangling from his lips, Rasputin held a map on the steering wheel as he weaved his rattling taxi recklessly through traffic. He narrowly dodged trenches in the rain-slicked street, and more than once I instinctively grabbed the dashboard as headlights bored down on us.

Stephanie and the children sat in the back seat, also without seatbelts and wide-eyed with terror. But we had saved $5, hadn't we?

Budapest is actually two cities: Buda—the more residential area—on one side of the Danube, and Pest—where most of the civic buildings are—on the other. Rasputin headed into the Buda side of the city, then twisted through the dark, tree-lined streets. A few times, he jammed the car in reverse and headed in the opposite direction. We weren't getting to our hotel quickly, but we sure got an idea of the impressive braking and acceleration capabilities of the Audi.

Suddenly, the car slammed over a speed bump. Our heads hit the ceiling. Before we'd settled back in our seats, Rasputin surged ahead, then hit the brakes again and opened the door.

We stood in the rain outside a small, brightly lit office as Rasputin hurled our suitcases to the ground. After collecting his fare, he roared off into the night.

"That was the most terrifying ride of my life," said Stephanie softly.

After checking the kids for any signs of whiplash, I walked toward the rental office. Inside, a huge guy with thick, black, wavy hair took our money in advance for the four-night stay and explained—in a booming basso profundo voice—how to get into the apartment. A few minutes later, we were walking up a narrow, weed-choked path toward our "luxury" digs.

The place had gritty marble floors, no heat, and smelled faintly of gas. In an effort to cheer the place up, someone had placed potted plants in strategic corners, but they were all dead.

"This is an 'executive' apartment?" Stephanie said.

"Kind of makes you wonder what an ordinary one is like, doesn't it?"

She wasn't amused. I wondered what company this phantom executive worked for. All I could conclude was that it wasn't in the Fortune 500.

At eight o'clock the following morning, after a fitful and uncomfortable night, we re-packed our suitcases and marched en masse down the lush, tree-lined streets of the neighborhood toward the rental service. We would not stay there another night. I felt like an idiot having paid up front for four nights and hoped to get a refund for the remaining three. Stephanie coached me to be firm and resolute with the rental agency—demand a refund. Don't take no for an answer, she said.

Along the way to the office—a few blocks from the dungeon—we spotted a charming, well-kept pension, the Buda Villa, set back amidst well-tended gardens. "Now THIS is the kind of place we should stay," said Stephanie.

"It's probably booked," I said. One reason I'd chosen the Executive Dungeon was because everywhere else seemed to be filled up.

"Let's at least check," she said.

Thinking it was a waste of time, I rang the buzzer anyway. To my immense surprise, a comfortable, two-room attic suite with a private bath was available, and it was only $90—the same as we'd paid for the dungeon. The cheery proprietor even agreed to let Kelsey and Drew play in the garden while Stephanie and I went to the dungeon's rental service to beg for a refund.

Approaching the office, we reviewed our grievances to list off to the owner. "It's just not acceptable," Stephanie said. "It's dirty, there's no heat, and it smells like gas."

"Yeah, the gas. I don't like that."

"Don't take no for an answer," she advised again.

"You sure you don't want to do it?"

"Yes." She pushed me toward the door.

Expecting to get a lot of shrugs and diversionary tactics from the clerk on duty, I pulled back my shoulders as I approached the desk. Lurch was still there. Maybe his voice was so deep because he never slept. "How was your stay?" he rumbled volcanically.

"Well, really, it... it wasn't acceptable," I reported. No sense in beating around the bush. I told him our various complaints, and he seemed truly taken aback. But he didn't directly offer a refund, so I opened up with the big guns. "And it smells like gas," I told him. At least I think it was gas. It could have been the rotting plants.

"Gas?" he said. "I'll have to have that taken care of right away." He tried to persuade me to take another room, but I asked for a refund. To my surprise, he agreed. Deducting only for the night we had stayed there, he handed over the remainder of the fee in Deutchmarks, the preferred "hard" currency in Hungary.

Back at the lovely Buda Villa, Drew asked, "So, how'd it go?" Drew always wants to know everything that's going on, and this time I was prepared for him.

"Well, I went up to the door, and the clerk totally ignored me; he looked through the glass like I wasn't even there."

"What did you do?"

"What d'ya think? I bashed in the door. Then I grabbed him by the collar and threw him over the counter."

"Really? So then he gave back the money?"

"Of course he did. He couldn't do it fast enough."

"Is this true, Mom?"

"Yes. It was incredible," said Stephanie, smiling.

I think Drew was a little disappointed when I told him the truth, but at least he knew he had a father who could imagine being such a tough guy.

Subject: (no subject)
Date: Tue, 12 May 1998 14:07:00
From: Chris Westphal
To: John Nava

Hi, John & Jessica,
Amazingly enough, our year is nearly up, just as we're learning our way around. We have dabbled from time to time with the idea of staying, but the work situation isn't ideal for me (which is certainly nothing new), or for Stephanie, who's grossly underpaid... so the coin flipped to make this decision toppled over on the side of "return," but just barely. If and when we do this again, it will definitely be two years or even three, and with real jobs lined up going in. Year one to learn the ropes, year two enjoy the place, year three to be an old hand.
Anyway, it's been a lot of fun, though sometimes quite difficult, but overall well worth it so far. Now that spring has arrived, we're already feeling nostalgic for Prague. We felt anything but in winter.
Tell us how things are in Ojai. Hope you survived the long wet winter, and that the kids are doing well.
Later,
Chris

When we finished getting settled in our new accommodations, the proprietor recommended a nearby restaurant, Szep Ilona. The place was within walking distance, and on the vine-covered patio there, we enjoyed a wonderful, leisurely lunch of spicy Hungarian food. Our Budapest vacation was looking better by the minute. We felt especially good knowing that we wouldn't be gassed to death during the night.

```
Subject: The ex-pat shuffle
Date: Sun, 17 May 1998 18:17:22
From: Chris Westphal
To: Tom Scarborough

Dear Tom,
In the continuing effort to drive ourselves insane,
we're once again considering sticking it out here for
another year. I'm scouting around for corporate writ-
ing work here that actually pays adequate money. As
for the general idea of staying: We're torn a thousand
different directions. One minute I'm in favor, the
next I miss friends & familiar sights, activities and
contexts in Ojai.
It was such an ordeal getting over here that to skip
town after we're just getting to know our way around
seems a shame. We'd also like to see more of Europe,
too. We hear great things about Turkey.
I would still have to land a job or have strong indi-
cations that one will turn up, in order to make it
work financially.
Well, sorry to sweep you into our turmoil. Hope all's
well.
Later,
Chris
```

The next morning, however, Kelsey came down with the sniffles, so she spent most of one day enjoying the luxury of American TV via Satellite. But when she was feeling better, we packed sightseeing into every available moment. Taking children to historic buildings and museums can be a chore, and though I won't claim that Kelsey and Drew were ecstatic about visiting such places as the decorative museum, they were attentive and patient just the same. The more active trips—a boat ride down the Danube and a "hop on/hop off" bus tour of Budapest—were a hit.

On the bus tour, while the bus stopped at a scenic vista overlooking the city, their stupid father watched as a con artist played a shell game. The con hid a wadded up piece of paper under one of three cups, then shuffling the cups around. Of course, this is the oldest rip-off in the book. Using gestures and a few words, the con bet a tourist to identify which cup the paper was under. The tourist won!

I moved closer. Now, the tourist was hooked. He doubled his bet. The cups were shuffled artfully around, and the tourist lost. He doubled his bet again, and I quickly calculated that it was about $400.

Now, the con artist moved in for the kill. The tourist lost all his money. I was completely amazed to watch this. I caught the eye of a bystander and rolled my eyes as though to say, "How gullible can people be?"

I was about to find out. The bystander sidled up to me. By now, another mark had appeared. My "friend" stood behind the con, pointing with his toe at the cup that had the paper under it.

Why, I thought, this guy is trying to help me. It didn't even occur to me that my new pal was a co-conspirator.

I got back on the bus a moment later, having lost all of the Deutschmarks I had gotten as a refund for the Executive Dungeon.

"You're kidding," said Stephanie after I'd confessed my foolishness.

"What did you do, Dad?" asked Drew.

"Nothing. I was stupid!" Now I knew how gullible a person can be.

Though I felt like an absolute idiot, I was determined to enjoy myself, and it wasn't difficult. We wanted to see as much as we could, and having lived in Prague for most of the previous year, we were well equipped to find diversions. We visited the opera house, the zoo, the decorative museum, and many other sites. But even if we had just gone from café to café along the Danube, it all would have been broadening in ways that can't really be calculated.

Stephanie and I loved the trip, but of course, as adults, we experience things with a certain distance. Children, on the other hand, are immersed in things, swallowed up by them. For them, walking through the streets of Budapest's castle complex or gazing upon structures such as the neo-Gothic parliament building, which has 365 towers, all of them looking like white frosting dripped from heaven, must be something like walking through a magnificent dreamscape. I like to think that their exposure to so many magnificent sights will help them appreciate the finer things, or at least not be too impressed by new shopping malls.

```
Subject: Terry-generated steam
Date: Thu, 21 May 1998 12:53:13
From: Chris Westphal
To: Cynthia Kear

Hi.
I had the temerity to not gleefully accept, without
question, Terry's parsimonious offer... which appar-
ently has sent him off into sulking silence. Or maybe
the people in the white suits came again, or he ran
out of medication. Sometimes he's lucid, other times
he's hovering somewhere over Jupiter.
Maybe we ought to form a support group for people
who've been Terryfied. Twelve Steps to a Terry Free
Life (which I guess I'm headed toward. But I've said
that before). Was Maxwell Perkins[10] like this?
-Chris
```

Living abroad with young children is almost a constant history lesson, too. In Budapest, Drew and Kelsey wanted to know about the 1956 revolution, about World War II, and about the Mongols and Turks who had sacked Budapest. Every experience—from a taxi ride to a museum visit—was an opportunity for learning.

Through the Eyes of Children

Stephanie and I found that the most important learning occurs almost without effort, though, because while living abroad, you are constantly immersed in different languages. Even if you can't understand what's being said, the foreign sounds are busy re-wiring your brain. Seeing such a variety of people surely makes you more accepting of differences among peoples, and hopefully, more tolerant.

---

[10]Legendary book editor for Ernest Hemingway, F. Scott Fitzgerald, and Thomas Wolfe, among others.

```
Subject: The plan - for the current nanosecond
Date: Wed, 27 May 1998 14:36:58
From: Cynthia Kear
To: Chris Westphal

Chris,
Well, seems like Terry has decided to defer a CA
launch. His e-mail oozed bitterness between the lines.
Despite his own efforts to the contrary, it's actually
a wise decision.
It's positively the same old same old. This time he
was trying to get an unsigned author in the Bay area
to set up a PO Box & send out mailers. What an impres-
sive mktg effort. Wharton¹¹ has things to learn, for
sure. Now, I appreciate guerilla mktg. But I think in
this case it's more like gorilla mktg and we'd all be
well served if he was caged.
Oy!!!
```

Through the eyes of our children, we saw everything on the trip with a more innocent eye. Budapest is deservedly famous for its fine restaurants, and every night we had dinner at a different restaurant, usually staying for several hours. But the children still craved familiarity, so we hit the Pizza Hut, too.

For seasoned travelers, eating at an American franchise restaurant is a no-no. But sometimes it's just the right thing to do. The truth is that, despite the chain's efforts to offer the same bland familiarity throughout the planet, a Pizza Hut in Budapest is not the same as a Pizza Hut in Los Angeles. The one we visited was decorated with a Hollywood motif, and the walls were covered with large black and white drawings of James Dean, Humphrey Bogart, and Marilyn Monroe. But their faces had distinctly, though subtle, Hungarian features. It was like a parallel universe Pizza Hut, where everything is off just enough to be disconcerting.

For three days we ran ourselves ragged around Budapest, usually returning to the pension past eleven. Then, in the comfort of our cozy attic, everyone on our bed, we'd watch Jay Leno or catch an American sit-com. Television was a little window on America. The shows seemed overblown and more banal than ever, yet they were also weirdly exotic.

I knew then that we had successfully detached ourselves from our country. After nearly 10 months abroad, we now floated weightless, immune to the gravity of our own culture.

[11] The University of Pennylvania's Wharton School of Business, consistently ranked as one of the country's best business schools.

The Kids Are All Right

One family's vacation is another family's living hell. Stephanie and I genuinely enjoyed traveling with Drew and Kelsey. It was wonderful to see the world afresh through their young eyes, and it made even the tedious things—such as a long train ride—more exciting. For them, ordering a snack from the porter was a great treat, and seeing them enjoy such simple things made every experience more meaningful.

Throughout our year, but especially while traveling, we did our best to treat Drew and Kelsey as partners in our joint adventure. That doesn't mean we catered to them. Rather, we were flexible when it came time to decide on an activity, and we solicited their input. In Budapest, for example, we perused our guidebook and let them select an activity or two themselves; they chose the zoo and a boat ride on the Danube. Stephanie and I got to pick the rest, including a bus tour of the city, a visit to the decorative museum, and a tour of the opera house.

Mealtimes can be particularly contentious issue when traveling with children, and there, we let them have some freedom as well. If we'd gone to lunch at a fancy restaurant that required Drew and Kelsey to sit still and be quiet for an hour or more, we didn't have any regrets about having dinner at McDonald's.

Our intention was to give the children the real sense that this was their trip, too.

There Is a Time for Everything... Usually

Later in the year, we took a three-week driving trip through parts of Italy and France. We were traveling in the high tourist season but had only made reservations in Venice, because otherwise we couldn't have found a place, and in France, where we had arranged to stay in a friend's apartment. Other than that, we were unscheduled. At first, not having a set destination at a set time was a little disconcerting, but ultimately it was liberating. When traveling, the only thing worse than being stuck somewhere you don't like is being scheduled to leave a place that you're enjoying.

The approach that worked best for us was to decide a day ahead where we would be going next. Referring to our guidebook, we'd find an appropriate hotel—or pension, usually—and make a reservation. Often, it took us a few tries before finding a place, but sometimes we were lucky on the first try.

Because of our lack of planning, we arrived in Sienna, Italy, the day after Il Palio, a yearly festival featuring as its highlight a no-holds-barred horse race right in the town's huge central square between riders from the town's 13 different districts. We missed the horse race—others told us later that the square was so packed with people that you couldn't see any of the action anyway—but we had a wonderful time just the same. The crowds had gone. It was easy to get a restaurant reservation, and by coincidence, the pension where we were staying was in the district that had won the race. There were celebrations, dinners, and boisterous parades throughout the area. We didn't get much sleep, but the spectacle made up for it.

We stayed an extra day in Siena, then later spent a week in Vernazza, one of the Cinque Terre, or "five lands," along the Italian Ligurian Coast. We then headed up to Lake Como and found it dreadfully boring, so we felt no regrets in leaving after one night.

Here are a few ideas to keep children involved and interested while traveling together:

- Get a good guidebook that lists activities for adults and for children, and solicit the children's input about what to visit. It's their vacation, too.

- Set reservations at extremely popular destinations, but otherwise consider letting your itinerary develop as you travel.

- Remember, every meal doesn't have to be a peak dining experience. Let the children pick where you'll eat from time to time—and don't be surprised if it's crepes from a sidewalk vendor. When it's time for them to shape up during a long and boring (to them) meal in a restaurant, remind them that they got to eat and do what they wanted, too. Now it's your turn.

- Let the children start a collection. Throughout the year, both Drew and Kelsey collected key chains. By the end, each of them had 20 or more from eight different countries.

- Bring snacks along for long travel times via train or car.

- Travel light, and ideally let your children handle their own suitcase. Both Drew and Kelsey have carry-on-sized wheeled suitcases.

- Keep a deck of cards, drawing materials, a mini chess set, or other diversions close at hand for long journeys.

- If you find an interesting historical tidbit in a guidebook, share it with them. For example, Drew and Kelsey were interested to learn about the pirates who invaded Lanzarote, about a medieval torture chamber we visited in Regensburg, Germany, and about Hitler's compound in the mountains near Salzburg.

The most important thing to remember is to be realistic and accept that you can't do it all. If a particular area is simply too packed with activities and sights to see, don't consider it a failure, but an opportunity to visit again.

ELEVEN

The Long Road Back

"You know you're an expat when... you no longer know the proper way to greet and part company."

—Jim Newman, Austria

Subject: no subject
Date: Fri, 20 Mar 1998 07:49:40
From: Chris Westphal
To: J.B. White

J.B. White wrote:
Come home, Westphals. No pretentious performance art here in America—just good, wholesome entertainment everyone can understand and appreciate. Europe is over. Come home, Westphals, come home.
Yep, that appears to be the plan. Had a chat w/ the co-owners of our rental property back in L.A. and they were extremely cool to the concept of our remaining on the continent any longer than absolutely necessary. They're tired of shouldering the managerial burden on their own. So, look for us in the first week of August! We'll be the ones with the strange-colored clothing, thick accents and suspicious attitude. Oh, that's the Czechs.
Later,
Chris

Like a Great Ship Changing Course

Toward the end of our adventure, our year abroad was like a great ship unable to change course once it was underway. Once the declaration had been made that we would stay for a year, it was almost impossible to leave early or stay longer.

If by some miracle I'd gotten a corporate job, we might have stayed. It would have meant more money, greater responsibility, and definitely less isolation. Unfortunately, by June we knew there was virtually no chance of that. We had to return home. A few days before the end of the school term, Stephanie was working when I went to the goodbye ceremony at the ISP.

I sat in the audience as each of the children who were leaving, including, of course, Drew and Kelsey, were called up on stage. I choked back tears as Drew stepped forward. He looked somber and subdued. I felt for him, knowing that he probably had unexpectedly had the best year of his young life. Kelsey looked typically cheerful. For her—more easy-going and in some ways less sensitive—I knew it would be easier to leave.

The fifth graders moving into sixth grade were given t-shirts and welcomed into Middle School, and I could see Drew's envy as clearly as though he held up a sign. These kids were going to a place he desperately wanted to go—deserved to go—and he was being left behind.

Later in the ceremony, the Sunshine Singers, of which Drew was a member, sang "The Rose," a song about taking risks in life and in love. The lump in my throat swelled as I listened to the song and heard Drew's clear and strong voice above the rest of the chorus. I felt like a monster, wrenching him away from his friends and from a context in which he was popular and successful. Right then, in the moment, I was bereft. I deeply regretted that staying in Prague was not as bright and realistic an opportunity for the family as it was for Drew. In a way, having to experience the pain and disappointment of leaving almost made me wish that we hadn't come at all. But we would have missed so much, and it was better to have enjoyed it and to have experienced it for a year than to have wondered about it for a lifetime.

We all knew that coming to a new country involved sacrifice. What we hadn't known was that leaving would also exact its price. Despite the fact that most of the year has been difficult—in many ways more difficult for me than for anyone, owing primarily to isolation—in the end, I knew it would have its rewards.

I knew that Drew and Kelsey would be stronger, more resourceful, well-rounded, and capable people because of this year. I knew that

Drew's sadness over leaving his friends would abate, and that he would renew friendships back home and make others. I hoped that his friendships in Prague would survive and evolve over time and distance, too. I knew that Kelsey discovered this year that she was stronger in academics and in the arts than she thought. She loved performing in the lavish school production of *The King and I*.

As the school ceremony ended, I was enormously proud of my children and all they had accomplished. I was also very proud of my family, because we had done what thousands just say they would like to do.

Afterward, in the familiar, airy lobby of ISP, it was the usual swirl of activity. Parents rushed after their children. Taxi drivers found their charges. Linden, the mother of Drew's best friend, Aaron, walked toward me. When she looked at me, she could barely hold back tears.

I hugged her. "This isn't easy." My throat was tight with emotion.

"No, it's not," she said. "I wish you didn't have to go."

"Me, too," I said sincerely. I didn't want to say anything more because I didn't want to start crying.

The children and I spoke little as we drove away from the school for the last time.

Stephanie still had two weeks of work left, and we were expecting another set of visitors, but in a way, we were already detaching ourselves from Prague as we prepared to return home. We had hoped that in our last couple of weeks there, the children could have a lot of play dates and gorge themselves on their international friendships. But within a few days of the goodbye ceremony, virtually everyone left. This was, to us, the previously unknown benefit of being "deep expats"—that is, people who live outside their home country more or less permanently: most of them go home for a part of the summer. Kelsey's friends Milena and Kim remained in Prague, so she was still occupied and entertained. But without Aaron, Drew was desperately bored.

After Stephanie finished with her teaching responsibilities, we traveled by rented car around Italy and France, doing the usual cathedral-museum-restaurant routine of tourists, though without any set itinerary. Some parents might think that traveling through Europe with young children would be a chore, but it was an absolute delight. In the year abroad, both Drew and Kelsey had grown more independent and self-assured, and we could see it wherever we went. They were comfortable on trams and metros. They were responsible about taking care of their suitcases as we moved from place to place. In the various cathedrals and other places we visited, they were quiet and respectful. Spending a week in Vernazza, one of the "Cinque Terre" on Italy's

Ligurian coast, Drew and Kelsey quickly found a group of children and played with them in city's labyrinthine interior.

Prior to going abroad, Kelsey and Drew seemed to be constantly sniping at one another, but they had undergone a magnificent change during their year in Prague. They were genuinely tender toward one another, happily posing together in Venice for pictures and playing with one another on the beach at Ville France sur Mer.

We spent a final few days in Paris doing more sightseeing, then flew back to Prague, exhausted. Waiting on the telephone machine was a message from a job recruiter at a Swiss company. Before going on vacation, I had seen their ad in the *International Herald Tribune* for a public relations and marketing writer, and I had faxed off a resume during my flurry of job applications and forgotten all about it.

Momentarily, visions of being an expat in Geneva danced in my head. Yes, I thought: a nice, modern apartment in the old part of the city, the kids in an international school, a decent car, and enough money to enjoy some of the finer things. I gave little thought to how we would handle business back at home, but knew only that some arrangement could be made. Switzerland sounded great to me. France sounded great. Anywhere sounded great so long as we could easily visit Prague from there and the position paid enough that we could travel and live well. I hurriedly called back the recruiter, but to my dismay, rather than the offer of an interview, I had the story of my life played back to me: the writing samples were great; the experience was interesting and compelling, but I didn't have enough corporate experience.

So, despite this last effort, we were going back to California. During our last two weeks in Prague, we concentrated on visiting our favorite sites: the wonderful Art Nouveau Lucerna theater, where you could take mixed drinks into the theater; Café Slavia, a noted meeting place for the arts and letters crowd; Palffi Palac with Eva and her family, where we sat outside on the balcony and enjoyed a meal that surely seemed terribly extravagant to the frugal Eva. We wanted to savor our Czech life and etch the exotic memories onto our brains.

When we weren't visiting these cherished places, I scoured local shops for sturdy boxes to hold the tremendous volume of possessions we had accumulated in a year: overcoats, a saxophone, Christmas toys, mountains of clothes, sheets, towels, liquor, small appliances that ran on European voltage, and a whole bowl full of Czech hellers (the near-worthless equivalent of a U.S. penny).

We gave most of the household goods to Peggy Krikava. Jim also had a Slovak congregation, and she would distribute the things to needy families. We had plenty of appliances waiting for us back in Ojai anyway. But wherever we looked in the apartment, there was more stuff to pack and never enough boxes to put it in. I took three separate trips to the airfreight terminal before we had finally whittled down our possessions enough to fit them into our original eight suitcases.

On our last evening in Prague, we went to our favorite family restaurant in Old Town Square. We wanted it to be a special evening, but soon Stephanie and I got into a serious argument about the vagueness of our future. We sent the children off to explore so we could speak more freely. Before we'd really gotten vicious, though, the children returned. They'd just met Anna Harris, a young woman who babysat for us back in Ojai. We were finished arguing and eating, so we followed the children to where Anna was in the square. She was obviously dazzled by the city. We told her how sad we were to be leaving and made various recommendations for what to see and where to go. Her enthusiasm for Prague made us still sadder to leave.

After chatting with her for a little while, we had to get back home. For the last time, we boarded the 22 tram that wound past the cobbled streets and the magnificent buildings, then wended up the steep cobbled road—called the Serpentine—past the castle and Strahoff Monastery. Finally, we took the short walk from the tram stop to Na Petynce and to our lovely apartment.

We had made arrangements for a driver with a van to pick us up at 4:00 the next morning and take us to Berlin, a five-hour drive, for the flight to Los Angeles. I had spent weeks making the flight arrangements, and this was the best I could do on our budget.

As I tried to sleep, I remembered the first night that we had spent in our first apartment. A huge thunderstorm had rolled in around midnight and woke both of us up. Stephanie and I went to the window, which looked out at Hotel Dum. Just as we were looking up, a bolt of lightning split the sky, lighting up the hotel eerily. I had been reading about Europe and World War II, and the thunder made me think of cannon fire. We were in this new place—a place that had seen a savage war. We weren't in California. This was all so bracingly different, so thunderously new.

"Are You Sure?"

And now it was over. We awoke at 3:00 a.m., and by 3:45 we were finished getting ready. I opened the door to take the suitcases outside and saw across the way two women getting out of a white Skoda. Hurriedly, they went to the trunk and pulled something out. Then, they unfurled a banner that read, "Are you sure?" It was Eva and her daughter, Tereza.

Indeed, we were not sure. We were not sure we wanted to leave, but we had to. We were not sure what we would do next when we arrived back in the U.S. But we were sure we were leaving just the same.

We gave Eva and Tereza the remainder of our excess: a clock radio, a VCR, a telephone machine, the liquor, and the bowlful of hellers. George, the van driver, arrived a moment later, and Eva warned him in Czech to drive very carefully. Quickly, we loaded our belongings into the van.

And then it was time to go. After some tears, hugs, and best wishes from Eva and Tereza, we climbed into George's van and were off. We drove past Terezin, the Nazi internment camp, then into the former East Germany. We wended through forested hills, past old villages. All of the scenery seemed like the end of a long and complex dream.

Dozing fitfully, we lurched over the uneven roads in the former East Germany and past the outskirts of the bustling city of Berlin, where huge complexes of panelaks still stood. Getting closer to the airport, the utilitarian panelaks were steadily replaced with ultra-modern buildings and congested thoroughfares.

Airports and airplanes blended together for us in our sad and tired state. After a hop to London, and a brief layover, we were back in L.A. Our friend, Sandi—the same woman who had seen us off exactly a year earlier—met us at the gate. It was almost as though she had never left the airport, but had spent the year circling it, waiting for our return. We were exhausted and numb from the journey. Los Angeles International Airport (LAX) seemed so jarringly loud, and as we circled around the airport headed for the freeway, it was disconcerting to be able to read the garish signs and understand what was being said on the radio. And those cars all around us were gigantic! The traffic didn't have anything on Prague, but how did people stand all the lights everywhere? Billboards, hotel signs, a strip club proclaiming "Nude Nudes." It seemed like too much.

We still had a two-hour drive home, so it was 10 p.m. by the time we pulled into Ojai. The shops were closed, the streets deserted. In 24 hours, we had passed from old world Europe to sleepy Ojai, and the contrast was jarring. Had we dreamed it all? Had a year really gone by that quickly?

Our home was still occupied by the tenant, so we reserved a motel room for this first night back. We fell onto the beds and went to sleep, exhausted from the initial re-entry into this country.

The following morning, Drew was off at 7 a.m. for Junior Lifeguards in Ventura; I'd arranged it from Prague. Kelsey called up an old friend and went over there to play. They hadn't missed a beat. Stephanie put me in charge of getting our cars started.

The AAA tow truck driver, who wore a name badge identifying him as Mike, met us at the motel and drove me to the house where I uncovered the cars. After a year of sitting, only one would start. When I mentioned to Mike that I needed to drive to the DMV to have the car re-registered, he cautioned that there was a good chance I'd get a ticket due to the car's expired tags.

"But I've got a truck," he said. "It's just sitting there at the shop. You're welcome to take it if you want. In fact, I don't need it 'til Monday, so just go ahead and drive it if you want."

I didn't take him up on it, but the offer alone—from someone who I'd never met before—was a fitting welcome home.

Comfortable Anywhere, At Home Nowhere

Time plays tricks on you when you're abroad. Or maybe the calendars are different. The first month you are there is a year long; the second is a week. The remainder of a year passes in a couple of days. Somehow, you've managed to squeeze a year of living, a year of new sights, sounds, tastes, and experiences, into a couple of weeks of real time.

As we entered our tenth month abroad, staying for just a year seemed too short. Not only had we made good friends in Prague, but we recognized that there was still much we hadn't done. It seemed a shame to have gone through so much preparation and disruption for only a year. Drew, who had vociferously resisted going abroad, now applied equal fervor to persuading us to stay. Kelsey, who for the first several months had pined for life back home, was now genuinely enjoying herself. Stephanie and I seemed to change our minds hourly. One moment, we craved friendships back home; we wanted to see the dog, enjoy familiar foods, make progress in our careers, such as they were. We recognized the extraordinary experience we had had and were prepared to resume our "real" life back home.

Then we'd reflect on the cultural wealth of Prague, on the new friends we'd made, and on the many opportunities we'd had to travel. What was our "real" life if not whatever we were experiencing? Why not just continue this and change our definition of who we were?

I tell myself that it would have been easy if I had a corporation telling me to stay or to go, but I didn't. Thanks to a stock market at home that seemingly knew no upper limit, as well as income from a rental property and other sources, we were maddeningly free to do as we chose.

We just had to choose.

For us as a family, going to Prague was the realization of a long-held fantasy. To us, living abroad meant many things, and it's difficult to list them in order of importance. A significant one, though, was a declaration that we weren't straight-jacketed by convention—that we were young enough to reinvent ourselves in the context of a wholly new culture. For me personally, with the publication of *Echo Valley* just before we'd left, it appeared to be the culmination of 20 years as a professional writer. I really thought that the publication of the novel and my unique opportunity to market it in Europe represented a great breakthrough. I was bitterly disappointed to be proven wrong.

Yes, the starting gun went off, but despite my greatest efforts, I never got out of the blocks because my publisher, Terry Harris, was a lunatic, a hopeless dreamer, or a crook. The great irony of the entire episode is that *Echo Valley* is about a writer, Tom Huttle, whose prospective publisher continually changes hands and whose dreams continually elude his grasp. Tom is expected to meet increasingly bizarre demands while his life unravels. I was living the life of my fictional creation with one crucial difference: Tom Huttle goes quietly insane.

I just got depressed. But unlike Tom, I had achieved a dream long held, and done it, despite many difficulties, splendidly well.

Expat Answers: *What personal qualities or characteristics do you think are most important for people considering living abroad?*

- *flexibility*
- *openness to new ideas, ways of life, people, and experiences*
- *tolerance*
- *willingness to give up the American viewpoint*
- *humility*
- *a non-chauvinistic nature*
- *gregariousness*
- *love of learning*
- *optimism*

–Various respondents

Life in the Rear View Mirror

If we had it to do over again, we'd likely plan from the outset to stay abroad a minimum of two years, with a break or two in the U.S. for rest and relaxation. Expatriates contacted for this book said almost universally that two years was a minimum. Writing from Japan, Pam Petrillo suggested two to four years abroad. "More than that and children start to see the foreign country as their home country," she said.

If you've never lived abroad, two years probably sounds like an eternity. But once you're there, it becomes your life. Sad as it may sound, your longing for things American (or Canadian, British, or Guatemalan) diminishes. As you're swept up by the daily concerns, frustrations, and wonders of life abroad, you step to the rhythm of your new country.

TWELVE

I Said Goodbye, You Say Hello

"You know you're an expat when... you feel like a tourist in your own country."

—Graeme Steel, Indonesia

Scanning the aisles in the supermarket a few days after our return, I was momentarily transfixed. These labels were in English. That fact alone seemed incomprehensibly weird, but when the clerk approached and asked, unsolicited, if I needed help, I was truly taken aback. "I… uh… rice. I'm looking for rice." Then she shocked me completely. With a broad smile, she said, "It's in aisle five. Can I show you?"

Can I show you? Had I heard right? She was going to walk me down to the aisle and point out the rice? Incredible! I didn't know what to make of this. Did I look *that* bewildered? "Uh…no thanks," I said. "I can find it myself."

In Prague, my limited vocabulary—and the generally surly clerks—usually prevented me from asking for help. Here, all I needed to do was look a little puzzled and they pounced on me, eager to help. The surreal experience continued at the checkout counter. The clerk gave me a cheerful "Good afternoon! How are you today?"

Caught off guard, I mumbled, "Fine." I hastily scrawled out a check, then instinctively moved to the end of the counter and started stuffing my purchases into plastic sacks. But a bagger quickly arrived. "Let me do that," he said helpfully. I stood there, marveling as he filled the sacks. But the courtesy offensive wasn't over yet; the bagger asked if I'd like help getting the groceries to my car. "Oh, that's all right," I said. "I can handle it."

"Wow!" I thought as I got back into the car. "Welcome back to America!" Talk about reverse culture shock!

Only after you've been away for quite a while do you realize how essentially pampered Americans are. Everything is designed to be more convenient, to offer you more choice—sometimes an avalanche of choice—and to make life easier.

Of course, all that choice has a price. There's advertising everywhere, and we're subtly, and not-so-subtly, encouraged to borrow, borrow, borrow so we can spend, spend, spend. And the engine of commerce has a tendency to wipe away anything that's old or independent—such as grand historic buildings, book shops, and mom and pop grocery stores—and replace it with something more economically efficient and, often, uglier and less personal. Nevertheless, if you can gird yourself against the hard sell, life in these United States has a lot going for it.

Still, it has its downside. In Prague, we were virtually forced to walk quite a lot, and as a result, we were fit and energetic on our return. In the U.S., we now had to drive to get anything done. In Prague, we were surrounded by splendid architecture, historic monuments, and cultural opportunities. In the U.S., we found concrete freeways and sprawling shopping malls. Instead of opera, symphonies, and elaborate marionette shows, we had movies. Culture was here to be found, to be sure, but now it took some hunting, especially in our small Southern California town.

They Think I Went to Guam

However, aside from all of the physical attributes and comparisons, the most striking aspect about our return was found on a more personal level. "Dad, the kids at school think I went to Guam!" Drew lamented one morning. "They don't even know where Prague is." I resisted the temptation to tell him that initially his mother hadn't known where Prague was, either. I said, "It doesn't matter, Drew. You know, and they're the poorer for not knowing."

The geographical ignorance of Drew's classmates was emblematic of a wider apathy that we hadn't really noticed before. Rudolph Papirnik, a friend in Prague, formerly worked for a large Chicago brokerage, where he had been amazed at how little interest some of his American co-workers had in travel. A training seminar was arranged in

Arizona, he said, and most declined, not because they didn't want to take the time or the training, but because they felt like Arizona was just too different from their daily surroundings. When Kelsey had to make a speech in class, I suggested she talk about her experiences living abroad. "Dad," she said. "No one cares."

Unfortunately, for the most part, that was true, especially for our children. Re-integrating was different for each of them. Kelsey, who had attended a small private school since the age of four, quickly got back into the social groove as though she had never left. It had helped that while we were away, she often wrote to friends. Also, though we were gone for a year, Kelsey's heart in many ways remained in Ojai. In some senses, I think this diminished her experience in Prague, but I don't think it's unusual at all. Though she had made close friends in Prague, I think she—as do many expatriates—held something in reserve, knowing that the situation wasn't permanent.

Drew, on the other hand, has more of a tendency to give his all. Initially, he had been adamantly opposed to going to Prague. While there, he was totally engaged not only in the academics, but in the social and political currents at school. When it came time to return to the U.S., he absolutely did not want to do so. Consequently, once we had returned, it took him a little while to adjust to life back home. He had had such a great experience abroad, largely because for the first time he felt like he had really been among many of his academic peers. It was difficult for him to put the year in perspective when he returned.

Fortunately, his sense of humor—a prime asset for anyone going abroad, even

MORE DATA, PLEASE... According to Michael Schell, a global relocation management specialist of Windham International, more than 40 percent of repatriated employees resign within two years of their return to the U.S. Scary statistics, but important to know.

TIP: Soon after returning home, visit favorite spots together as a family. Recall the experiences you had overseas together, and reflect on the changes you've undergone as a family.

TIP: To help your children integrate their expatriate experience into their lives, help them decorate their rooms with memorabilia, photos, and artwork from countries you visited.

children—proved to be his route to social acceptance. At lunchtime, he emceed "The Drewie Show," a parody of daytime talk shows in which he would interview classmates. Who was popular? Who was "going out" with whom? These were exactly the things with which his classmates were most concerned—and exactly the things with which he had lost touch.

He had soon attained that elusive quality known as "popularity." He was 11 1/2 when we returned and at the threshold of adolescence, when blending in with the crowd—whether it was in the clothes you wore, the slang you used, or the attitude you affected—sometimes became all important. Sometimes, the slightest variation from the fashion of the moment meant social isolation.

Drew was not immune to these influences, but the year abroad had reinforced, not weakened, his individuality. The popularity he enjoyed—and continues to enjoy—didn't require him to sacrifice academic achievement or to become some kind of fashion clone. On the contrary, his classmates respond to him because he is a bit iconoclastic, both in his worldview and his humor.

No Place Marker Held Our Spot

I wished Stephanie and I could just tell a couple of jokes and return to where we left off. However, not only had we changed, but "where we left off" was no longer there. No place marker held our spot while we were away. People moved on, and their social orbits evolved as they got involved in different things during our absence. Ironically, we, who had been so intent on breaking the routine of our previous lives, craved a return to the way things used to be. We had wanted to escape our own ruts, yet we wanted everyone else to remain in theirs while we were gone. Of course, they had not accommodated this unspoken wish.

To make matters worse, many seemed oddly disinterested in our experiences—and among returning expatriates, we're not alone in this complaint. I don't think it's as simple as disinterest, however. I think it's more the case that the returning expatriate has a great need to talk about the experience—a greater need to talk about it than others have a need or desire to hear about it. To be fair, the disinterest goes both ways.

For example, I didn't want to hear about all the political switch-backs that had happened in the school district while we were away. I'd listen to a recitation about that for about as long as a friend would listen to me talk about editing the *Slovak National Healthcare Newsletter*.

Other friends seemed to believe that living abroad for a year was just a long vacation. Yes, we'd been to seven different countries; yes, we'd suffered cathedral overload and gotten lost in several different languages... but that was only a small fraction of the experience. Adapting to life—ordinary, day-to-day life, with all its quirks and rough spots and petty annoyances—was the real experience.

No one really wanted to hear how triumphant we felt when we'd first been able to go up to the window at a tobacconist and buy a three-month transit pass because we had acquired so many little bits of knowledge over time. We had to know that you got a steep discount for buying three-month's worth of stamps for our transit passes. We had to know when the stamps went on sale. We had to know how to fill out the transit pass itself. We had to know that the stamps were available at tobacconists, and we had to know how to ask for them. You're probably bored already, just reading about the stupid transit pass, but you see what I mean—living abroad is not the same as being a tourist.

So perhaps people's attitude toward returning expatriates isn't disinterest so much as an inability to relate. It's as though you've somehow become an alien being. Over time, though, common experiences tend to bridge the gap, but not always. Regardless of how diligent you've been with e-mail, phone calls, and letters, some friendships will die, some will be rekindled, and new ones will be made.

I think every expatriate faces anxiety about returning home. A month or so before we left Prague, I went out for beers with Jim Krikava. He wanted to tell me the story of how he had come to Prague as a missionary. Jim is a great storyteller, and I listened with rapt attention as he told a tale of being betrayed and later ousted from his ministry after he disclosed the infidelity and financial misdeeds of another pastor. Over the previous seven years, it had been a great struggle for him and his wife to overcome these difficulties. Ultimately, he had found a new sponsor and found a new congregation—the church we attended in Prague.

Jim said they planned to return to the U.S. within the next couple of years, but he was concerned that when they returned, no one would understand—or care—about their experiences as an expatriate.

"I don't really know what it'll be like," he said. "I don't know who I'll be able to relate to anymore. I'll want to hang out with people like you, who understand what it's like, and I don't know where I'll find them."

The apprehension that Jim has about finding a way to fit in again is reasonable. He may find that few are interested in hearing about what, to my mind, is a story of a family's remarkable strength, character, and courage. The Krikavas still don't have to face that eventuality, because at this writing, they remain in Prague, happily ensconced at ISP and in the midst of buying a house. But it is something that they will know to prepare for. Two of their daughters attend university in the U.S., so they will be able to learn from their experiences in repatriation as well.

In expatriate forums on the Internet, you can't read about the experience of repatriation without noting a sense of bitterness. In the work environment, co-workers don't value expatriates' experiences abroad or understand the hardships they faced. They may be jealous or competitive or simply uninterested. Meanwhile, office politics and power relationships may have changed dramatically. Often, returning expatriates find it impossible to re-integrate into their old workplace, and they move on. I think it's because they've grown in terms of their experiences, their independence, and their problem solving abilities.

I hope no one goes abroad just to have good tales to tell. People with this motivation are tourists, out to snap pictures and make lists of places visited, cathedrals toured, and knickknacks bought. Expatriates are a different breed entirely, holding in common a desire to expand their world, to embrace it and to experience it for what it is instead of imagining or being told what it might be. The desire to live abroad is an internal drive that can't be satisfied with any number of public television travelogues or *National Geographic* magazines.

Ultimately, personal growth—not career growth (though it is definitely a factor)—is the best reason to go abroad. Though the experience itself is wonderful, even when it's horrible, it's what goes on inside you that has lasting meaning. Outside of your normal context, you may be able—perhaps for the first time—to see new aspects of yourself.

At the beginning of this book, I wrote that "Why not?" was as good a reason as any to go abroad, but I must revise that assessment. There are dozens of other solid "whys" for a family to undertake such an adventure. The greatest of them, though, is that life is short. It's short no matter what plans you make, what career ambitions you have. It's short whether you are educated or ignorant. But it's richer if you claim your dreams.

Getting Back into the Groove

Preparing to live abroad usually takes many months, or even a year. Yet returning to the U.S. is given little thought. We buy the plane tickets, pack up our stuff, and go, expecting to fit right in. However, it makes sense to spend considerable time strategizing your return. Make school arrangements, financial arrangements, and housing arrangements well in advance. This is one reason that only a year abroad is simply not enough.

To make your transition back to life in the U.S. less stressful, here are a few do's and don'ts:

- **Don't** compare life in the U.S. with your life abroad. As in the opposite case, it simply doesn't matter how it's done overseas.

- **Don't** spend too much time telling people about your adventures abroad.

- **Do** make time to maintain contact with overseas friends and colleagues or with other returning expatriates.

- **Do** consider and give value to the ways in which you've changed, both personally and professionally.

- At work, **do** list problems that you overcame, lessons you learned, and skills you strengthened while living overseas.

- **Do** offer to share your insights and knowledge with other employees who may be assigned to an overseas office.

- **Don't** be too frustrated if your insights and initiatives are not immediately embraced. You've had a long time to develop them, but in a context quite separate from the one you now occupy.

- **Do** update your résumé to reflect professional and volunteer experiences you had abroad.

- **Do** give yourself some time to adjust to the pace and tone of life in the United States prior to launching a job search.
- **Do** get involved in your community. Your new knowledge and the flexibility and resilience you have learned by living abroad give you significant new strengths to tackle challenges in many areas of life.

Expat Answers: What are some things that would make repatriation easier for children?

- *Line up a list of friends to visit, and tell the children not to boast about their experience abroad.*
- *Send them to a small school.*
- *Be prepared for the fast pace of American life—the dependency on items of convenience.*
- *Set a daily routine.*
- *Accept the fact that people will not know how to deal with your broader view and understanding of the world. They'll get bored with your stories and think you are bragging about how well-traveled you are when you are only talking about what you have experienced and what you did.*
- *Keep up to date on fashions and activities.*
- *Be ready to feel uninformed about local issues.*
- *Don't be afraid to ask for help from everyone—neighbors, friends, shopkeepers, etc. And don't be embarrassed about it.*
- *Children need to know that they count and that their feelings and thoughts are part of the moving and living experience of being an expatriate.*

–Various respondents

THIRTEEN

I Do Declare! I Have Nothing to Declare

"You know you're an expat when... you can only remember how to tell military time."

—Michelle Jones, Japan

A month or so after our return, we got a notice in the mail from the U.S. Customs Service that the boxes we had airfreighted from Prague had arrived in the U.S. and were waiting at the airport. I drove the two hours to the KLM Cargo terminal at LAX, thinking that our several boxes had been inspected by the guys in the black suits and fedoras and gotten a disinterested sniff from a drug-detecting German shepherd. I figured all I had to do was write out a check for the duty, load the boxes, and be on my way. I hoped it would be that way, because I had an appointment that afternoon and had little time to spare.

When I got to the cargo terminal at the airport, however, all I got was a form with instructions to go to the customs office a few blocks away. I thought this meant I was really going to get the full treatment— meticulous examination of every knickknack and boot, every pencil and gewgaw under a microscope. In short, I thought I was in for a deluxe tour of something Kafka might have imagined, up to and including an interrogation under glaring lights. I knew I'd crack, and I had nothing to hide!

TIP: If you are shipping personal belongings to the U.S. from abroad, indicate on the U.S. Customs form that they are "Used Personal Belongings." The duty, if any, will be significantly lower. If your belongings are not so labeled, U.S. Customs may charge duty on the items based on their value as new—even if you bought them in the U.S. and are sending them home.

MORE DATA, PLEASE...
It's fascinating reading... well, no, it's not, but it's good stuff to know, especially if you're shipping lots of stuff. The U.S. Customs bureau's Web address is www.customs.ustreas.gov.

At the customs office, though, I just had to stand in line for about an hour. Finally it was my turn, and I handed over copies of the customs declarations that I had filled out in Prague when the boxes had been sent.

The customs official referred to a reference manual intriguingly named the *Harmonized Tariff System,* or (naturally, they use the acronym) the HTF. The book, according to the U.S. Customs Bureau Web site, "is the size of an unabridged dictionary." And about as interesting to read, I'd bet. To quote again from the Web site: "Experts spend years learning how to properly classify an item in order to determine its correct duty rate. For instance, you might want to know the rate of duty of a wool suit. A classification specialist will need to know, does it have darts? Did the wool come from Israel or another country that qualifies for duty-free treatment for certain of its products? Where was the suit assembled? Does it have any synthetic fibers in the lining?"

Well, we were guilty in the wool department. Both Stephanie and I had bought big wool overcoats in Prague, and they were in the boxes. Should have worn them on the plane, I now realized. Did they have darts? What's a dart? Did the wool come from Israel? I didn't know, but the customs agent didn't ask.

Somehow, though—without looking at the coats—he calculated that we owed about $80 each in duty on them. I guess he really had studied the HTF. The saxophone? No duty on that. It was a piece of junk anyway, so I was pleased about that. Because I had been kind of vague on the customs form, listing items such as "household goods," the customs agent trusted my memory and my honesty as to the contents of my boxes. I suppose he could have gotten suspicious and ordered a thorough inspection of each box, but thankfully he didn't. That would have required even more time, because the boxes were still in the cargo warehouse at the airport.

All in all, our customs bill was about $200—most of it owing to the overcoats. It was more than I expected, but I was willing to be a good sport about it. I pulled out checkbook, ready to get it over with.

"Cash, certified check, or postal money order only," I was told. That's probably in the HTF, too.

"But…" The IRS takes checks! The Post Office even takes checks! But there was no arguing with him.

The window was going to close in half an hour, so I had no time to waste. I ran back to the car and made a frantic tour of LAX and environs, looking for an ATM machine. Finally, I found one in a traffic-snarled shopping mall and got the cash.

I made it back in line, and after waiting there for a few more minutes, I handed over the money just before closing time. The customs agent stamped the paperwork in strategic places, and I rushed back to the freight terminal where the warehouseman found all the boxes for me.

However, it was almost two years before we opened the last of our boxes, so I guess I needn't have been in such a hurry.

Mailing vs. Shipping

Ever wondered what the difference between shipping and mailing is? Well, I didn't either. But knowing the difference could save you time and money. According to the U.S. Customs Bureau, mail—whether

MORE DATA, PLEASE… KLM Cargo is one of the largest air-freight companies in the world, with an air network reaching some 150 countries. Their Web site is www.klmcargo.nl.

TIP: It's illegal to bring into the United States any drugs or prescription medication not approved by the U.S. Food and Drug Administration—even if you have a prescription for it in a foreign country where it is legal.

TIP: If you plan to bring home merchandise purchased abroad, wait until late in your stay and have the merchant ship it directly. It will still be subject to customs, but you'll have insurance from the shipper. If you paid for the merchandise with a credit card, you may have some protection against defects and breakage.

TIP: If you're using airfreight to ship less than 100 kilos, it might make sense to declare the weight at 100 kilos in order to get the lower rate. As the saying goes, "Do the math."

it's letters, raincoats, or tubas—is sent via the international postal system, which is run jointly by international governments. Shipping, on the other hand, is via private carriers, such as an airfreight company.

Commercial shippers—FedEx and UPS, for example—use customs brokers to do the paperwork to get shipments through customs. You pay a little extra for that service. On the other hand, the U.S. Postal Service works directly with customs. In other words, if you use the postal system to send things home, you don't have to pay the customs broker. You will have to pay a small customs handling fee, however.

Emery Worldwide offers services including airfreight, ocean shipping, customs brokerage, and logistical support for large shipments. It has offices worldwide, and is on the Web at www.emeryworld.com.

Most airlines also offer airfreight services. Unlike postal delivery, airfreight services—such as KLM Cargo and Emery—deliver from airport to airport. That is, they don't deliver directly to your home, which is the reason I had to go to LAX to pick up our belongings.

When we were packing up our belongings in Prague, we kept coming up with more stuff to ship. I'd take one huge box down to the freight terminal, fill out the International Customs Declaration form, pay the freight, and then go home. A few days later, we'd have another box, and I'd go through it again.

However, I could have saved a lot of money if I'd been more patient (Note to self: This is an important thing to remember in all areas of life!) and waited until we had everything packed and then made one trip to the airfreight terminal. The reason is that the greater the weight of the total shipment—not of each individual box—the lower the per-kilo rate. For example, with KLM Cargo, a shipment from Los Angeles to Amsterdam weighing less than 100 kilos (220 pounds) costs $4.40 per kilo. A shipment weighing more than 100 kilos costs just $1.85 per kilo. At 500 kilos, the price drops to just $1.70 per kilo. (Rates from foreign countries to the U.S. vary.) So it would have made more sense for me to mail all of the boxes at once and pay a lower rate.

FOURTEEN

Expat Light: House Exchanges

We had plunged into our year abroad with both feet. Our home was rented and all of our belongings, except for what we carried in our suitcases, were in storage. To us, the "point of no return" was reached even before we left the U.S.

But many prospective expats may not be quite so intrepid. Most expatriates recommend taking a reconnaissance trip to your destination country prior to actually moving there. Although this option wasn't financially feasible for us, it's a good thing to consider. If you choose this route, one of the best ways is through a house exchange. This will give you the opportunity to familiarize yourself with your prospective location while enjoying the convenience of living in a home and, depending upon the arrangements you make, having use of a car.

Home exchanges are typically arranged through any of a number of exchange facilitators. Most home exchanges are for periods of two to four weeks, but longer or shorter periods can also be arranged. A home exchange is as near as you can get to being an expatriate without having to send out a bunch of change-of-address cards.

The Internet is an ideal tool to help you arrange an international house exchange. Various companies operate searchable Internet databases that allow you to key in your destination city and narrow the search by different exchange criteria, from a straight swap with both families changing places to a long-term rental.

Exchange companies are not active parties to the exchange. All they do is provide contact information and the listing. It's up to you and the family you exchange with to determine exact dates and limitations, if any. You are responsible for plane tickets and any visa arrangements. The exchange company will generally supply an exchange agreement, and if you have specific restrictions—such as no pets, or no one under 25 driving the Ferrari—then that's the place to list it. Formal contracts,

TIP: Prior to commencing your exchange, secure critical information, such as credit card and bank account numbers, either in a locked drawer or a file cabinet in your home or in a safety-deposit box at your local bank.

though, are rare, because when all is said and done, a home exchange is a matter of trust, not of contractual obligation.

Choosing an Exchange Company

You can log on to various exchange companies and search their listings free of charge, but in order to list your home or get contact information for homes that are listed, you have to pay an annual membership fee. Depending on whether your listing will appear only on the Internet or will be in published catalogs along with the Internet, fees range from $30 to more than $100, but don't let this nominal cost stand in the way of selecting what you think will be the company that best suits your family's needs.

To list your home, fill out a detailed form—either via fax, mail, or on the Internet. You have the option of including a picture or two with your listing, too. All sorts of homes are exchanged, so just because you have a rather modest home doesn't mean no one will be interested. Be honest and thorough in your listing, and don't fail to mention nearby attractions and amenities.

Don't be overly enchanted just because a company has a nifty presence on the Web. Before joining, make sure that the exchange company you use also publishes a conventional catalog. Not everyone is active on the Internet, and sometimes browsing through a catalog will help you find a prospective exchange in a city that you otherwise might not have considered. If the country you want to visit is off the beaten track, you may want to join more than one exchange organization.

There are many advantages to a house exchange, with economy and convenience being among the greatest. Traveling with a family and staying in hotels can be not only expensive, but also exhausting. But by living in a house or apartment, you have the advantage of being settled, having a fully equipped kitchen, and enjoying all of the other amenities of home. With the money saved in accommodations and car rental, it's easier to take three- and four-day jaunts to outlying areas—and to enjoy more extravagant diversions, if so desired.

TIP: Prior to the exchange, arrange for a friend or neighbor with common interests to welcome the exchange family. It will give the exchange family a link to the community and give you an added safeguard in case something goes wrong.

A Few Do's for House Exchangers

The following tips will make your house exchange easier:

- Start your search at least six months prior to your planned exchange.
- When you're considering an exchange, be as flexible as possible about dates, length of stay, and location. The more flexible you are, the more choices you'll have to find what you want.
- Make a contingency plan that goes into effect should there be an emergency on either side. Since travel arrangements might already have been made, this plan makes sure that the exchange family will have your house in any event, and vice versa. Lori Horne, co-owner of Intervac U.S., who has done with her family 20 house exchanges, recommends that if you can't get this type of assurance from an exchange family, don't go through with the exchange.

MORE DATA, PLEASE...

Intervac, established in 1950, is the largest home exchange organization, boasting 11,000 members in 50 countries. France and the U.S. each represent about 18 percent of their listings. Contact them on the Web at www.intervac.com or at 30 Corte San Fernando, Tiburon, CA 94920, Tel: 800.756.4663.

Vacation Homes Unlimited, operating since 1986 with listings in 40 different countries, is on the Web at www.vacation-homes.com or 16654 Soledad Canyon Road, Suite 214, Santa Clarita, CA 91351, Tel: 800.848.7927.

- Stay in regular contact with your exchange family before the exchange to discuss all of the details. E-mailing makes this easy and allows information to be written down. Because of language differences, confusion can arise, and you don't want to receive a shocking call the day before you leave telling you that your exchange family thought the exchange was scheduled for a different time.
- Leave specific information for the visiting family regarding activities, sights to see, and entertainment, as well as the location of the supermarket and other conveniences. Leave maps, guides books, and other materials. Ask your exchange family to do the same for you.
- Organize in a notebook detailed instructions about things you find simple but a foreign family might not understand, such as how to use the washing machine, how to turn on the pool motor, how to run the air conditioner, etc. Ask them to do the same. You don't want to spend a month in someone else's house and not know how to wash your clothes.
- Leave names and numbers of neighbors, in case your exchange family has a minor problem, such as how to operate an appliance or where to go to buy pet food. Inform you neighbors about the exchange before you leave so they won't think something is amiss.

- Be open and honest regarding things such as smoking, pets, allergies, and the exchange of cars.
- Try to meet the family at the beginning of the exchange and/or at the end. This gives you an opportunity to develop more of a personal relationship with them.
- Leave one drawer empty in every room where visitors will be sleeping. In closets, leave room for 10 or so empty hangers.
- Lock or store especially valuable or delicate items in a safe place—particularly if the exchange family has small children. Theft is virtually unheard of, but accidents do happen.
- Give yourself at least 48 hours to get over the jet lag and get your bearings before formulating any opinions about your exchange location. It will be different, and it will take some getting used to.

More Benefits of House Exchanges

Another benefit of doing a house exchange is that you'll get an opportunity to live a normal life while in the new country. Often, exchange families arrange introductions to friends and neighbors. You'll also get a chance to enjoy activities, shops, and entertainment that are not on the typical tourist agenda. A house exchange is much more like living in a foreign country than visiting it, and more often than not, exchange families develop social friendships, visiting one another frequently as the years go on.

It's up to the exchange families to determine that they're receiving an even trade, and many factors come into play in making that determination. Typically, if your profession or income is comparable, and the size and general location of your homes is comparable, it's a good match. However, you may want to experience a different kind of life and find a family willing to make that exchange. For instance, if you have a house in a semi-rural area, you may be able to make an exchange for a smaller apartment in Paris, Rome, or London.

One obvious concern about home exchanges is safety. In other words, are you going to come home and find out that all your furniture is down at the local flea market? According to exchange facilitators, serious problems are extremely rare. You have to bear in mind that the other family is also trusting you to take care of their house. Demographics play a role, too. Most families who do exchanges are established, over 40, and have children. As a member of that demo-graphic, I have to say that the idea of traveling to another country in order to rifle through other people's underwear drawers would be a lit-tle absurd.

The exciting topic of homeowner's insurance always comes into play, and fortunately with exchanges, it's fairly straightforward. Check with your insurance provider, but generally, homeowner's insurance will be unaffected due to an exchange. Most auto insurance policies allow for other drivers for periods of 30 days or less. As with any trav-el, it's wise to make sure your medical insurance will cover you while you're abroad.

FIFTEEN

A Host of Student Exchange Programs

When I was in high school, one of the seniors was an exchange student from Sweden. He was tall, had long curly blond hair, and spoke with an accent. All of the girls seemed to be crazy about him. His stay had been arranged through AFS, the American Field Service, the grand-daddy of exchange organizations.

Founded 53 years ago, AFS is still in business and now offers not only student exchanges, but a variety of work-study opportunities, internships, and other programs as well. Affiliated with partner organizations in 44 countries, AFS-USA sends approximately 1,700 U.S. high school students abroad annually. Costs depend upon the program chosen, but typically a U.S. family will pay around $5,000, exclusive of airfare, to send a child abroad for a six-month stay. The child is fully insured and is given a small amount of spending money. A volunteer host family supplies room and board, and the exchange student lives as part of the family and attends either public or private school.

AFS isn't the only game in town, however, and if your family isn't in the position to travel abroad for an extended period, your child can do it through any number of international exchange programs.

The Rotary Foundation, a part of Rotary International, sponsors a variety of Academic Ambassadorial Scholarships for university undergraduate and graduate students, providing funding for one academic year of study in another country. The awards are up to $25,000 and are intended to help cover round-trip transportation, tuition, fees, room and board expenses, and educational supplies. Nearly 1,000 awards were given for study in 2000-01.

MORE DATA, PLEASE... AFS operates 125 different programs for students, teachers, and others. On the web, they are at www.afs.org/usa, or Tel: 800.237.4636.

MORE DATA, PLEASE... En Famille is on the Web at www.enfamille.com or can be contacted at 26 Savarias, 33240 Salignac, France, Tel: (from the U.S.) 011.33.557.435.248, Fax: (from the U.S.) 011.33.557.433.955. En Famille is not a member of the ECA or CSIET, but is admitted to various European organizations of a similar nature.

Rotary's Cultural Ambassadorial Scholarships are for either three or six months of intensive language study and cultural immersion in another country and provide funds to cover round-trip transportation, language training expenses, and home stay living arrangements, up to $12,000 and $19,000 respectively.

Until 1998, AFS and Rotary were about as far as my knowledge of exchanges went. Then, a few months after we returned from Prague, Carol Johnston, a colleague of Stephanie, told us about En Famille, a French organization that arranges linguistic-cultural exchanges for children between nine and 13 years of age. Carol and Bruce Johnston had already hosted a French child, Sara, for six months. Sara attended the local junior high school and got along famously with the Johnston's two daughters, Emily, then in seventh grade, and Blaire, who was in fifth. At the end of Sara's stay in the U.S., Emily went to France, where she stayed with Sara's family for six months. Not to be outdone, Blaire went to live with another French family for the same period. Both were having a wonderful time.

We asked Drew, then 11, if he would be interested in living in France for six months, and he was immediately enthusiastic. To us, his enthusiasm was both rewarding (our year abroad as a family had truly made him a more adventuresome and confident person) and terrifying (how could we let our baby go abroad for so long?). When the Johnston's daughters returned from their stay, they were fluent in French and, more importantly, linked with a foreign family and a foreign culture. By then, the director of En Famille, Jacques Pinault, had interviewed Drew, Kelsey, Stephanie, and me, and the arrangements to send Drew to live in France were well underway.

Despite the thorough application, the Johnston's experience, and the interview with Jacques Pinault, Stephanie and I still had second, third, and nineteenth thoughts about sending Drew. We knew he could get homesick. He could get ill. He could just plain be miserable. But Drew was now unwaveringly determined to go, and in our final analysis, Stephanie and I felt it would be wrong to deny him such a remarkable opportunity, which offered so many positive possibilities for his future. He was particularly excited about learning French, which he had studied while in Prague.

In September 1999, Drew and I boarded a plane at LAX to Paris and spent the weekend with Drew's French family, the Lagouttes. Over the course of those few days, the reality of what he was about to do sunk in for him. One afternoon, sensing that Drew was desperate to talk to me alone, we took a walk in the countryside together. "I wish I'd never seen that brochure," he said. "I don't know how I ever thought this was a good idea."

We Would Always Wonder

A part of me wanted to take Drew home immediately, but I knew that he and I would regret it if I did. I said, "Drew, before we went to Prague, we felt the same way. We didn't know if it was a good idea to go or not. It's always like that when you tackle something big. And we could have changed our plans and stayed home. But if we had, we would not have that incredible experience to look back on, and we would always wonder, 'what would have happened if we'd

> **MORE DATA, PLEASE...**
> Applications for Rotary's Ambassadorial Scholarships are available from most Rotary Clubs. Listings can be found in your local telephone directory. For complete eligibility guidelines and other information, log on to the Rotary Foundation's Web page, at www.rotary.org/programs/amb_scho/index.htm, or contact Rotary International at One Rotary Center, 1560 Sherman Avenue, Evanston, IL 60201, Tel: 847.866.3000, Fax: 847.328.8554.

MORE DATA, PLEASE... For a broad overview of exchange organizations, as well as links to various agencies that are involved in cultural and academic exchanges, take a look at Student Exchange Net, at www.studentexchange.net. There, you'll find many resources valuable to families involved in exchange programs.

gone?' If you don't go through with this, you'll have that same thought. You'll always wonder."

"I know, Dad, but, I'm gonna miss you guys so much," he said, his voice cracking with emotion.

"Oh, we'll miss you, too. Every day. But we're going to be there every second, thinking of you and loving you. This is going to be a part of your growing up. You are going to find that you have strength you didn't even know existed, and I know you can do it. I just know it."

I then related a story told to me in Prague by a friend, Jaroslav Najman. After the Warsaw Pact countries invaded then Czechoslovakia in 1968, Jaroslav escaped to Sweden. Though he arrived with nothing "except a leather jacket," financial need was not the greatest challenge he faced. "I couldn't speak to anyone," he told me one afternoon. "I never knew before how much status—power, influence, respect—that language gives you. In Czech, I was intelligent, clever, well informed. In Sweden, I was nothing.

"People dismissed me and had no interest in me because I couldn't communicate with them. This hurt me a lot. I felt like I was worthless. But then I started to learn Swedish, and the more I learned, the better I felt. And when I finally could speak the language, I felt better than I ever had. I could say to myself, 'I know your language. And I also know my own. I have something that you don't have.'"

You'll Always Be Able to Look Back on This

I told this to Drew, and I said that when his six months were over, he would have not only a new language and all of the benefits that come along with being bi-lingual, but also a relationship with a new family and a new culture. Most importantly, I said, he would have learned about himself. "For the rest of your life, Drew, when something is difficult for you, you'll be able to look back at this and say, 'I learned a foreign language. I came to a new country and I made my way there, and whatever I do from now on will not be as difficult.'"

The following morning, I stood with Drew outside the small Catholic school that he would attend for the next six months. And all of my fears and misgivings about sending him abroad on his own seemed frightfully accurate. Drew, the boisterous, confident child I had flown over with now looked pale and withdrawn. The little French he knew from his study in Prague had evaporated.

I toured the campus with him very briefly. Then, as classes were about to start, I gave him a big hug, more words of encouragement, and still more hugs as he clung to me. And then I left, and I didn't turn around to wave at him one more time because I didn't want him to see the tears streaming down my face.

I was absolutely consumed with worry as I boarded my flight back to California, and I wasn't much reassured when we called Drew that Sunday. He was desperately homesick. He spoke in a faint voice, hardly able to form the words through intermittent tears. We called weekly, and for the first few weeks, his voice quavered, and he com-

TIP: Various exchange programs, information, and discount travel for students and teachers are available through the Council on International Educational Exchange, on the Web at: www.ciee.org or by calling Council Travel at 800.226.8624.

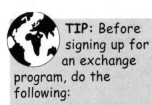

TIP: Before signing up for an exchange program, do the following:

- Check references and groups to which the exchange organization belongs.
- Speak with families and children who have participated.
- Arrange a personal interview with the organization's coordinator or director.
- Make sure the host family abroad has been visited and evaluated by representatives of the organization.

If your young child is then involved in an exchange:

- Go with your child when he or she goes abroad, and visit with the family.
- Communicate regularly with the host family.
- Trust the host family to be responsible, as you will be responsible for their child.

plained that he didn't understand a word that was said in class or with the Lagouttes. In addition, he was accustomed to being a top student, but he was now completely adrift. Though he never asked to come home—we would have been hard pressed to refuse—he was absolutely miserable for the first five or six weeks, despite the Lagoutte's best efforts to console him.

But then he dug deep within himself and he found a well of determination and focus that even he didn't know he had. In three months, he was up to the class level in his studies. In five months, he was reading the *Harry Potter* books in French. At the end of the exchange, he got the best report card in his class.

He came home a new child, brimming with a new type of confidence. He had always been a confident child, and even more so after Prague, but sometimes that confidence arose because things were easy for him. Now he had succeeded in meeting a very difficult challenge. What Jaroslav had said was true, with some modification. Drew did indeed have something that others didn't have, and he was justifiably proud of it. But along with his new confidence also came something equally as important—a new humility, and Jaroslav hadn't mentioned that. Drew knew what it felt like to be dismissed, ignored, and at times, ridiculed. So his six months abroad expanded his world, and it also expanded his heart in ways that we could never have predicted.

For the past six months, Lauren Hoffmann, Kelsey's 10-year-old French "sister" has been living with our family in an exchange also arranged by En Famille. The youngest in her family—a "late hatch," as a friend in Prague would put it—Lauren is a sweet and accomplished girl, playing the flute and ice-skating competitively. These months have been rewarding for all of us as we've seen her progress steadily in English. She has now reached the point of being quite fluent and is reading at or above her grade level.

While having another child live with your family is wonderful and rewarding, it is not simple. Kelsey and Drew were often jealous of the attention we gave Lauren—especially when she started calling us Mom and Dad.

In a couple of weeks, it will be Kelsey's turn to live with Lauren's family in France for six months. We will miss her terribly, and as with Drew, we are letting her go with misgivings. Kelsey was enthusiastic about going to France early on, when the trip was still theoretical. Now, however, as the day of her departure nears, she is scared and worried. Sometimes, we wonder what in the world ever possessed us to sign her up. Then, we look at Drew and at Lauren and see the remarkable growth both of them have achieved, and for a while—at least until Kelsey comes into our room unable to sleep for worry—we think it's a good decision. Still, we can't wait for it to be over so we can look back at it and say to her, "Now, aren't you glad you did it?"

Naturally, it takes a strong and mature child to embark upon this type of exchange. Being cut off from your native language is an enormously stressful experience, and certainly not every child could, or should, endure it. I don't think that it is something that should be done without the child's enthusiastic agreement, at least at the outset. Cold feet are to be expected; Stephanie and I had a severe case before leaving for Prague, so maybe it runs in the family, or maybe it's just normal.

> **MORE DATA, PLEASE...**
> The ECA, formerly known as the U.S. Information Agency, can be reached on the Web at http://exchanges.state.gov, or contact the Bureau of Educational and Cultural Affairs, U.S. Department of State, SA-44, 301 4th Street S.W., Washington, DC 20547, Tel: 202.401.9810, Fax: 202.401.9809.

MORE DATA, PLEASE... CSIET is on the Web at www.csiet.org, or contact the Council on Standards for International Educational Travel, 212 S. Henry Street, Alexandria, VA 22314, Tel: 703.739.9050, Fax: 703.739.9035, E-mail: mailbox@csiet.org. To order the Advisory List, send a request and a check for $15 (VA residents add 4.5% sales tax), or call the numbers above and provide credit card information. Overseas orders for the Advisory List cost $20.

Exchanges with young children carry with them lots of emotional freight. Since 1978, En Famille has facilitated more than 1,000 exchanges, mostly between France and Great Britain, and France and Germany. Our friends, the Johnstons, were in fact the first North American family to participate. Statistically, it's worth noting that in all of those exchanges, En Famille founder and director Jacques Pinault has had only a handful of problems that required a child be sent home.

At any age, children who participate should have a great amount of courage and self-sufficiency, and such exchanges serve to strengthen those traits. As part of the exchanges in which we have participated, we've hosted both Lauren and Arnaud, who is Drew's French "brother." Both children lived as part of our family, pitching in with household chores, traveling with us, and in all ways being a part of the family. Both did very well in school—Arnaud with some prodding—and completed their stays here highly competent in English.

Foreign students coming to the U.S. have something of an advantage because English has become a de facto international language, and most have studied it already in school. The advantage of exchange programs at younger ages—before the age of 13—are manifold. First, language acquisition is much easier, and the child is less likely to have an accent. Drew has no American accent in French, for example, and is often asked which area of France he comes from. Younger children also blend in more easily with classmates and with the family; perhaps because they have less of a separate identity and less mobility than older children. Lauren, for example, calls Stephanie and me Mom and Dad. Lastly, school performance is less important at younger ages. Often, U.S. students who study abroad in high school suffer because they miss core curriculum classes back home. Consequently, they sometimes don't graduate with their class or have to attend extra sessions to make up the missed work.

MORE DATA, PLEASE.... The Federation of International Youth Travel Organizations, FIYTO, is on the Web at www.fiyto.org.

Get 'em, FIYTO!

While personal references are important, it's helpful also to be familiar with the various U.S. groups and agencies that oversee exchange programs. Knowing that a given exchange program has complied with the requirements of various organizations can go a long way toward putting your mind at ease. Here's a brief rundown of agencies that have a role in overseeing or regulating international exchange programs in the U.S.:

ECA: The Bureau of Educational and Cultural Affairs (ECA), formerly the USIA (U.S. Information Agency) is part of the State Department and is the regulatory agency that keeps an eye on exchange programs in terms of their compliance with immigration law, visas, etc. U.S. Student Exchange programs have to be registered with the ECA or they can't issue the cleverly named IAP-66 (soon be given the mellifluous moniker, the DS-2019) form. This form is needed for foreign exchange students to get a J-1 visa in their home country. The ECA also oversees the Fulbright and other programs for graduate and undergraduate students.

CSIET: The Council on Standards for International Educational Travel (CSIET) is a not-for-profit organization that establishes standards for programs operating international educational travel and exchange programs at the high school level. It monitors compliance with those standards and distributes information regarding international educational travel organizations. Every year, CSIET publishes the Advisory List, a compendium of information about various exchange organizations that is distributed to high schools and host families. Only organizations that comply with CSIET standards are listed.

FIYTO: The Federation of International Youth Travel Organizations (FIYTO) is a worldwide, non-political, and non-sectarian travel trade association for people in the travel industry. FIYTO is an advocate for young travelers, working to ensure that they obtain flexible, affordable travel and travel-related services. It is more concerned with the travel aspects of student exchanges than the nuts and bolts of arranging or overseeing them, though many exchange organizations are also members of FIYTO.

The Host with the Most

All acronyms and affiliations aside—and those above are only a fraction of those that dip their spoons into the lucrative exchange pie—getting involved in a program is as easy as picking up the phone and calling the local high school. Many high schools already participate in foreign exchange programs, and one of the easiest ways to get involved is to host a foreign student. Typically, you're asked to provide room and board for a visiting student over a period of six months, but sometimes for a whole academic year.

During the exchange, you have the option to be in close contact with the foreign student's family abroad. If they're anything like us, they'll call every week. Often, if the exchange goes well, the foreign family will then offer to host your child in their country. You'll be responsible for getting a visa and assuring that proper insurance is provided for your child since this may not be an official exchange through a program, but the personal relationship you'll have with the foreign family is better than all the acronyms and official oversight in the world.

Even if a mutual exchange doesn't occur, your family will have had the experience of seeing and, in some respects, experiencing a foreign culture. It is rewarding, but not always easy. Drew and Kelsey were often jealous of the exchange students we hosted, because the visiting children needed and got more attention from Stephanie and me, particularly early on. In En Famille's literature, parents are strongly advised to treat the visiting child like any other member of the family. This is easier said than done, especially at the beginning of the exchange when we tended at times to be more empathetic with the visiting child, recognizing the fact that they needed more attention.

Sending our children on international exchanges and hosting foreign children in our family was among the most difficult and at the same time most rewarding experiences of being parents. To watch your children leave, knowing that what they're doing will be stressful, lonely, and difficult, is immensely difficult. Waiting for their safe return is agony, and Stephanie and I both spent many sleepless hours concocting disaster scenarios in our heads. Fortunately, we rarely shared them, and none of them came to pass.

But the end result—a more accomplished, confident, and compassionate child who has solid links to another family and culture—is a tremendous reward. In the years to come, as our children apply for college and start their careers, I have no doubt that their ability to speak a foreign language and their familiarity with other cultures will be invaluable to them.

When Arnaud left, concluding Drew's exchange with the Lagoutte family, both Stephanie and I looked back on that eventful year. "It's hard to believe that it's over," I commented.

"Amazing," said Stephanie. "It went by so fast, now that we're at the end of it."

"But Drew did a remarkable thing," I said. "He could have *not* done it and not have had those experiences, and the year would still be over. Look at how much more he was able to gain."

"It's true," said Stephanie. "It's true."

APPENDIX I

Your Bags Are Packed, Your Days Are Numbered

Our preparation to spend a year overseas took about a year—one reason that, in hindsight, we felt a longer stay abroad would have been wiser. Depending on your situation, your planning may take less than a year, but it shouldn't take more. The lists below are in our sequential order, but you don't necessarily have to complete them in the order listed. Some steps take longer than others.

Forms and Paperwork

Leaving the U.S. is relatively simple, but getting into another country—particularly for a stay of three months or longer—can be a bureaucratic nightmare. Of course, entry and visa requirements vary by country, so it's very important that you learn as much as you can ahead of time. Without a visa, three-month stays are permitted in the Czech Republic. One way to stay longer is to periodically go to an adjacent country—Germany or Austria, in the case of the Czech Republic—and get an exit stamp on your visa. You can take care of it in a weekend and then are permitted to stay in the Czech Republic for another three months.

Of course, doing one-day trips to Germany every 90 days is easy when you're a student or single teacher. Doing it with a family can have be an ordeal. Fortunately, Stephanie's school helped her get her long-term residency permit. As her spouse, I was eligible as well, although I had to do the paperwork for myself and for the children.

Wherever you go, here are the things you must accomplish prior to departure:

TIP: Rental applicants should pay a fee for a credit report at the time they submit a rental application. Review the credit report with your real estate agent, and call all references and former landlords yourself.

Ninety or more days prior to departure:

- Make sure your passports are up to date and won't expire while you are out of the country.

- Contact the consulate of your destination country and find out residency and visa requirements.

- Apply for an International Drivers License (available at AAA offices).

- If you intend to take a pet with you, contact the consulate and find out the requirements. Some countries, including Japan and England, require quarantine periods that can last as long as six months, during which time the pet is probably caged most of the time. If that is the case in your destination, seriously consider giving your pet away, or at least having it stay with another family at your expense.

Thirty days prior to departure:

Assemble the following documents and make at least two copies of them. Give one copy of everything to a trusted friend or relative. CARRY the original documents with you. Each spouse should also carry one set of copies on the plane. Do not put originals or copies in your checked luggage.

- Birth certificates for all family members.

- Passports for all family members.

- Passport photos (12 or more copies for each person).

- An immunization record noting vaccination records for each family member (available from your physician).

- Marriage license (available from the Vital Records Department in the county where you were married).

- Copy of physician's report for most recent physical (have a physical prior to departure).

- Diplomas and certificates for any educational programs you have completed.

- Driver's license.

- Baptismal certificates, if any, for your children.

- Recent report cards for your children.

- Recent résumés.

- Letters of recommendation from employers or teachers.

- Recent brokerage statement.

- Recent bank statements.

- A list of all bank, credit card, and brokerage accounts, along with contact phone numbers and addresses.

- Veterinary records, if you're taking a pet.

- Any other document which could possibly be of value abroad and the loss of which would be troublesome.

TIP: Contact local schools and colleges to find out if they have visiting professors coming to your area. They could make excellent short-term tenants—with their rent payment guaranteed by the school.

TIP: Get a good phrase book for the language of your destination country.

TIP: Get post-cards and maps of your home-town. They're great for students to share with their classes.

Home, Here, and Abroad

Finding a home is hard enough when it's in the same town. When that home is halfway around the world, it's almost impossible. Unless you're able to make a reconnaissance trip abroad and spend several weeks looking for a home (see Chapter Fourteen for more details)—with no guarantee that you'll find one—it's probably best to try and find a temporary place to stay, such as a bed and breakfast near work or school, while you house hunt.

Your immediate concern in this country will probably be renting your current home. If you've never dealt with rental property, the task can seem overwhelming. I've owned and sometimes managed rental properties for more than 20 years, and I would strongly discourage doing it yourself. The risks of something going wrong while you're away are too great.

Four to six months prior to departure:

- Ask friends for recommendations of real estate agents who can help you lease your home. Find out how long the agent has been working in your area and whether he or she intends to stay for the foreseeable future. Ask for references, and follow them up.

- When you've selected a real estate agent, ask him or her if there are any improvements you should make to the property prior to advertising it for lease.

- Make any necessary repairs to your home, especially those that are a matter of safety, such as broken steps or railings, faulty electrical systems, or malfunctioning glass doors.

Ninety days prior to departure:

- Have the HVAC (Heating, Ventilation, Air Conditioning) system checked and serviced.

- If your house is on a septic system, have the tank pumped and inspected.

- If your yard is landscaped, now is a good time to consider installing an automatic irrigation timer. Tenants are less likely to be diligent about turning on and off the sprinklers than you are.

- If you don't already have one, consider hiring a gardener to maintain the landscaping in your absence.

- Start advertising your home for lease now. Be aware that finding a tenant for just one year is sometimes difficult and can take a little while.

Sixty days prior to departure:

- When you've approved a tenant and gotten a move-in deposit, thoroughly inspect the property with the tenant and the real estate agent. Note the condition of each room, and make sure the tenant signs this inspection document. Keep a copy in your files and give another copy to the real estate agent.

- Modify your homeowner's insurance, if necessary.

TIP: List the important goals that you plan to accomplish while you're abroad. What will they mean personally? Professionally? Spiritually? In terms of your relationship with your family? The longer and the more detailed, the better.

TIP: With your family, watch films made in your destination country. Naturally, stick with comedies and lighter fare.

- Open a joint bank account with yourself, your accountant or trusted third party, and the property manager (most likely your real estate agent) as signers. All transactions concerning your home—including the mortgage, tax, and insurance payments—should be made through this account. With on-line banking, you can easily check deposits and withdrawals, make deposits, and transfer funds. You'll also have a clean record of rental-related expenses for tax purposes.

- If you're not taking your pet with you, arrange to place it with another family either temporarily or permanently.

For your destination country:

Finding housing abroad is often just good timing. When we arrived in Prague, rents were extremely high due to an influx of foreign workers—mostly American executives and their families. Our local contact helped us find an apartment, but we regretted our choice three months later due to the apartment's distance from the children's school.

By that time, the rental market had softened up considerably, more apartments had been renovated to "western" standards, and a lot of corporations were pulling out of Prague for economic reasons.

Tips for finding housing in your destination are covered elsewhere in this book, but here is a brief checklist:

Ninety days prior to departure:

- Network in the U.S. to find reliable real estate service companies in your destination city.

- Network with other contacts in your destination city to learn about desirable neighborhoods and to get help in finding temporary quarters on your arrival.

- If you can make an advance "reconnaissance" tour of your destination city, do so at least two months prior to your family's arrival.

On arrival:

- If you haven't already chosen a home prior to arrival—and this will probably be the case—plan to spend 30 days or more in a hotel or bed and breakfast while you look for housing. Use this time to search through neighborhoods that are near to work, school, and conveniences such as grocery stores and public transportation.

- Network with other expatriates as much as possible to learn about available housing.

- Make sure your house or apartment has an operating telephone already in it.

- Don't let your budget be your sole guiding force in choosing a home. It's more important that it suits your family's needs.

TIP: Getting children involved in the move is important so that they have a sense of excitement and interest—even though they don't have control over your destination. Here are a few ideas:

- Read travel stories about your destination country.

- Watch documentaries and travelogues together.

- Listen to music from your destination country.

- Search the Internet for information on your destination country.

- Using magazines, newspaper travel articles, and other sources, work together on a collage about your new country.

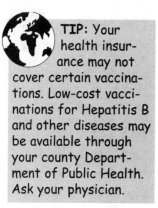 **TIP:** Your health insurance may not cover certain vaccinations. Low-cost vaccinations for Hepatitis B and other diseases may be available through your county Department of Public Health. Ask your physician.

Work

If you plan to work while abroad—and at least one person in your family probably will—you may be in a position to be transferred overseas by your company. If that's the case, a lot of the more difficult tasks—such as finding housing, getting your kids enrolled in schools, and getting a residency permit—will probably be taken care of for you by a corporate relocation department. If you think you may be a candidate for an overseas transfer, find out whether your company or another in a similar field has an overseas office that you might be interested in joining.

In addition:

Find out what kinds of compensation packages are typical for overseas transfers in your field through an employment consultant or other contacts.

If you need additional training to secure an overseas position, start that process as soon as possible.

If you're interested in teaching English while abroad, find out what certificates are accepted in your destination country. In most European countries, the RSA-Cambridge Certificate is highly sought after.

If you plan to learn the language, get a set of language tapes. They're great to listen to in the car.

Whether or not you intend to work while overseas, the people within your current company can be a valuable resource in terms of networking. It helps to have at least a few contacts in your destination country to help you find your way around.

Education

Living overseas isn't so much about geography as it is about learning. You'll need to prepare your children for their upcoming adventure—and prepare yourself as well.

Six months prior to departure:

- At your children's school, see if the teacher can help you set up pen pal relationships in the destination country.
- If you'd like to start a distance learning program while abroad, such as an MBA, look into the programs that are available in your field.
- As a family, read stories, fables, and other material from and about your destination country.
- Investigate U.S. Overseas Schools in your destination country. (See Appendix II for information for the State Department's Office of Overseas Schools.)
- If you're interested in your children attending local schools in your destination country, inquire at the country's U.S. Consulate to find out the requirements.

Health and Emotional Preparation

Moving abroad is a romantic notion, giving you an opportunity to redefine yourself and your family in a whole new context. While you contemplate the idea of living abroad, consider the dreams that such an adventure can help you achieve. Will it make you a more interesting person? Will it broaden the perspective your children have on the world? Will it renew your marriage and strengthen your family? Will it help you capture within yourself some spirit of adventure and passion that's been dulled by the day-to-day concerns of ordinary life?

Indulge your imagination in answering these questions. Idealization is your friend, and when you're mired in the practical concerns of visas, moving, and renting your house, these initial fantasies will propel you forward.

Moving abroad is something like writing a book—it helps to have a powerful vision of what it will be like when it's finished or else the drudgery of actually making it happen becomes overwhelming.

As a family, discuss your perceptions of the world and your place in it. How will having a broader understanding of the world benefit you and your family? Ask your children what they think about the idea of living in another country. (They may hate it, so be prepared.) Would they like to learn another language? Are they interested in other cultures? Have them make some lists regarding what they want to do or accomplish while living abroad so that they have some goals as well.

Once your decision to move abroad has been made, and even after you're committed to going, you'll still wonder whether you're doing the right thing. You know you really can't turn back now, but perhaps you wish you could. When these feelings start to overwhelm you, look back on the list you made of your personal goals. These are the real reasons you're going; all of the preparation is just the price you have to pay first.

In the final analysis, moving abroad is less about geography than it is about you and your family's journey in life. Consider the most challenging thing you've ever done. Maybe it was starting a business or a new career, raising children, or getting over a rocky spot in your marriage. Though these things were difficult and perhaps sometimes seemed impossible, the rewards likely extended far beyond the actual task and led to greater personal development than you might have imagined. Remind your children of times when they've faced difficulties—maybe a good friend moved, or they started in a new school, or they had a teacher they didn't like. But they found new friends, they adjusted to the new school, they found a way to deal with the teacher. Make sure you treat their fears and worries seriously, and give them the encouragement they need for this life-transforming chapter in their lives.

Other important steps to take include:

- Every member of the family should have a complete physical before going abroad.

- Six months prior to departure, find out from the consulate of your destination country what vaccinations and other inoculations are recommended. The Centers for Disease Control and Prevention also provides this information.

- Get vaccinations appropriate to countries you *may* visit while abroad.

- From your physician, get a supply of often-used medications, such as prescription asthma or allergy medications. Your doctor may have to write multiple prescriptions for these items.

- Purchase a one-year supply of over-the-counter medications that you're likely to use while overseas. However, be aware that some over-the-counter and prescription medications permitted in the U.S. are illegal in other countries, and if you try and bring them in, you may run into trouble. Check with the consulate of your destination country and then find substitute drugs that are similar and legal.

Finance and Insurance

A great deal of preparing to live abroad is essentially figuring out how to maintain your life back home. In whatever ways possible, it's important to put your domestic existence in suspended animation, ready to be re-animated quickly on your return one, two, or more years in the future. But you have to do it in a way that allows you maximum freedom overseas.

Ninety days prior to departure:

- If you don't use Intuit's Quicken, Microsoft Money, or a similar computer banking program, get one and start using it.

- If you don't have a credit card issued from a U.S. financial institution, get one now. For the sake of convenience, one that allows you to download transactions over the Internet is best.

- Through your insurance broker, research and revise homeowner's, auto, and other property insurance as necessary.

- Research available expatriate health and accident insurance policies. Make sure that whatever policy you acquire has a simple claims procedure, allowances for repatriation in the case of severe illness or catastrophic accident, and of course, reasonable deductibles and limits.

- Tell your credit card companies that you will be abroad for an extended period of time. Otherwise, they may think someone has stolen your card, and they might freeze your account.

Sixty days prior to departure:

- Have your will and/ or family trust updated.
- Have bank and brokerage statements forwarded to your accountant or other financial adviser.
- Have your accountant or a trusted friend or relative added as a signer to at least one of your accounts. In case of emergency, they can make a payment.
- Find out from your credit card company what insurance is provided automatically when you rent a car overseas using their card. Often, rentals over 30 days are excluded from coverage, so inquire specifically about these limits. You'll also need to know deductibles, claim procedures, exclusions, and other restrictions.
- With your mortgage lender, open tax and insurance impound accounts for your home mortgage. It will cost you a small amount in lost interest, but give you a lot of security.

Thirty days prior to departure:

- Close and consolidate bank accounts that are seldom used.
- Get new ATM cards, and make sure the PIN numbers are 4 digits. It isn't a bad idea to get an extra ATM card or two, in case the magnetic strip wears out while you're away.
- Get a small amount of currency for your destination country, enough to get you settled on the first day or so. One hundred to two hundred dollars is probably adequate.

- You may want to get enough traveler's checks to tide you over until you see a paycheck overseas. However, with the availability of ATMs, we found traveler's checks to be more bother than they're worth. In any event, make sure you have some reserve to get you past the first few weeks, whether it's in the form of cash, traveler's checks, or funds in an account that you can access via the ATM.

- Make a thorough list of all bank, credit card, and other accounts. Include account numbers, international and domestic contact telephone numbers, and mailing addresses.

APPENDIX II

It's All in the Web... Somewhere

The Internet provides a staggering number of resources for expatriates. I used it extensively in gathering information for our trip abroad and for this book. I also solicited input from other expatriates by posting a questionnaire on my Web site and distributing the link via various expatriate message boards.

When noting a Web site in the book, I tried first to use those that were sponsored by a governmental entity. My second choice was large corporations and non-profit trade groups. My last choice was small companies, not because I didn't trust them, but because I'm reluctant to include information for an institution that may change dramatically or cease to exist. Small companies that are included here have been, to the best of my knowledge, in business for a number of years and are likely to remain viable. However, I don't make any representation as to the reliability of their services.

Some Web sites exist solely or primarily on the Web, either as databases or link sites for other services and products. The only way to contact them is via the Internet or e-mail. Other sites are components of conventional businesses, and consequently also have physical addresses and telephone numbers. If this is the case, I've included that information.

Following, in alphabetical order, are Web sites that were mentioned in this book or others of interest:

AirSafe.com provides airline safety data and information.
www.airsafe.com

American Field Service (AFS) operates 125 different programs for students, teachers, and others.
www.afs.org/usa
Tel: (Toll-free in the U.S.) 800.237.4636

American Medical Centers operates medical centers in Eastern Europe that offer "western" style medical care. Their Web site also features links to other travel health related sites.
www.amcenters.com
American Medical Centers Management Co., Inc.
143 Newbury Street, 6th Floor
Boston, MA 02116-2925
Tel: (from U.S. or Canada) 877.952.6262
Tel: (from all other locations) +1.617.262.5301
Fax: +1.617.262.5302
E-mail: headquarters@amcenters.com

The American Moving and Storage Association provides tips, checklists, and other information pertaining to interstate—not specifically international—moving.
www.moving.org

Appliances Overseas features a wide range of adapters, TVs, and other appliances that will work worldwide.
www.appliancesoverseas.com/

Bankrate.com helps you find the best interest rates for credit cards or for any other type of borrowing, from mortgages to car loans.
www.bankrate.com

BigStep offers Web site building tools, instruction, and free Web page hosting.
www.bigstep.com

The Bureau of Educational and Cultural Affairs lists and oversees accredited student exchange programs.
http://exchanges.state.gov
Bureau of Educational and Cultural Affairs
U.S. Department of State
SA-44, 301 4th Street S.W.
Washington, DC 20547
Tel: 202.401.9810
Fax: 202.401.9809

The Centers for Disease Control and Prevention provides a searchable database with complete information about required vaccinations, health alerts, and other travel-related health concerns worldwide.
www.cdc.gov/travel
Centers for Disease Control and Prevention
1600 Clifton Road
Atlanta, GA 30333
Tel: (Toll-free in the U.S.) 800.311.3435
Tel: (International) +404.639.3534

The Central Intelligence Agency *World Factbook* is huge database including maps, histories, and exhaustive data about almost everywhere on earth.
www.odci.gov/cia/publications/factbook/index.html

Cheap Tickets.com is an on-line travel service where you can book discount air travel, rental cars, hotels, and other travel services.
www.cheaptickets.com

The Council on Standards for International Educational Travel (CSIET) is a not-for-profit organization that establishes standards for organizations operating international educational travel and exchange programs at the high school level.
www.csiet.org
CSIET
212 S. Henry Street
Alexandria, VA 22314
Tel: 703.739.9050
Fax: 703.739.9035
E-mail: mailbox@csiet.org
To order the Advisory List, send a request and a check for $15 (VA residents add 4.5% sales tax), or call the numbers above and provide credit card information. Overseas orders for the Advisory List cost $20.

Council Travel offers discount air and travel services, plus a variety of exchange programs for teachers and students. To use Council Travel, you have to prove you're a teacher or student and purchase an identity card from them for $22.
www.ciee.org
Council Travel
205 E. 42nd Street
New York, NY 10017
Tel: (Toll-free in the U.S.) 800.226.8624

DirectMoving.com features links to dozens of overseas and domestic house-finding services, plus a vast amount of other information and links.
www.directmoving.com

The Embassy Network has contact information for every country.
www.emb.com

Emery Worldwide offers services including airfreight, ocean shipping, customs brokerage, and logistical support for large shipments. Offices worldwide.
www.emeryworld.com

En Famille facilitates family-to-family exchanges for students 9 through 13 years of age.
www.enfamille.com
En Famille
26 Savarias
33240 Salignac
France
Tel: (from the U.S.) 011.33.557.435.248
Fax: (from the U.S.) 011.33.557.433.955

Escape Artist features articles and links about overseas investment, retirement, tax havens, and other expatriate resources for disenchanted Americans.
www.escapeartist.com

Expat Access provides information about expatriate organizations and clubs and offers other services.
www.expataccess.com/General/Organizations.shtml

Expat Exchange features links and information about movers, freight shippers, etc., plus message boards frequented by expatriates.
www.expatexchange.com

The Expat Post features resources, forums, and entertainment for the professional expatriate.
www.expatpost.com

EXPAT WORLD is a newsletter of international living, featuring links and message boards on various topics of interest to the expatriate.
www.expatworld.net

The Expatriate Group, Inc. is a Canadian firm offering services
for Canadians working, retiring, and investing overseas.
www.expat.ca
The Expatriate Group, Inc.
Suite 280
926 - 5th Ave. S.W.
Calgary, Alberta
Canada T2P 0N7
Tel: (Toll-free in North America) 888.232.8561
Tel: (International) +403.232.8561
Fax: (International) +403.294.1222
E-mail: expatriate@expat.ca

The Federation of American Women's Clubs Overseas, Inc.
is an international network of 78 independent clubs with a combined
membership of over 16,000 women in 37 countries worldwide. It
serves as a support network for American women living and working
abroad and is particularly active in the fields of U.S. citizens' concerns, education, environmental protection, and women's and children's rights.
www.fawco.org/index.html

**The Federation of International Youth Travel
Organizations (FIYTO)** is a world-wide, non-political, and non-
sectarian travel trade association.
www.fiyto.org

Free Web Preview has links to services that provide free space for
Web pages, plus free Web site building tools.
www.fwpreview.com

HomeSchool.com has general information about home schooling,
questions and answers, links to home-schooling related sites, and a
full line of curricular products and K-12 home-school courses.
www.homeschool.com

Information about various issues of concern to the expatriate family,
including safety and medical issues, job-hunting, and repatriation.
http://intljobs.about.com/careers/intljobs/cs/familiesabroad/index.htm

Intervac is the world's largest home exchange organization.
www.intervac.com
Intervac
30 Corte San Fernando
Tiburon, CA 94920
Tel: (Toll-free in the U.S.) 800.756.4663

Johns Hopkins Center for Talented Youth features math and
writing tutorials for students in sixth through twelfth grade.
www.jhu.edu/gifted
Johns Hopkins University Center for Talented Youth
3400 N. Charles Street
Baltimore, MD 21218
Tel: 410.516.0081
Fax: 410.516.0200

Kallback offers economical "callback" international telephone service.
www.kallback.com
Kallback
417 2nd Avenue W.
Seattle, WA 98119
Tel: (Toll-free in the U.S.) 800.516.9992
Tel: (International) +206.479.8600
Fax: (Toll-free in the U.S.) 800.516.9993
Fax: (International) +206.479.0009
E-mail: info@kallback.com

KLM Cargo is one of the largest airfreight companies in the world,
with offices in 10 major U.S. cities and an air network reaching some
150 countries.
www.klmcargo.nl
KLM Cargo
11001 Aviation Blvd., Suite 216
Los Angeles, CA 90045
Tel: 310.646.4010

The Living Abroad International Resource Center features information and services for visas, work permits, security, housing, insurance, international schools, taxation, everyday life, health care, and other issues for 96 different countries.
www.livingabroad.com/index.html
Living Abroad
32 Nassau Street
Princeton, NJ 08542
Tel: 609.924.302
Fax: 609.924.7844
E-mail: info@livingabroad.com

Medibroker International is a fully independent British expatriate medical insurance broker offering free quotes for Expatriate International Health Insurance via the Internet.
www.medibroker.com
Medibroker International
17 Seatonville Road
Whitley Bay, Tyne & Wear
NE25 9DA
UK
Tel: (In the U.K.) 0191.297.2411
Tel: (International) +44.191.297.2411
Fax: (International) +44.191.251.6424
E-mail: medibroker@aol.com

Oanda.com operates a quick, easy-to-use currency converter for 164 currencies in use throughout the world—everything from Afghanistan Afghanis to Zimbabwe Dollars. It also offers an on-line expense report management system and other services for travelers and business users.
www.oanda.com/convert/classic

The Office of Overseas Schools, under the U.S. State
Department, administers the overseas schools used by American
diplomatic personnel. This site also provides links to teaching pro-
grams and other information about overseas education.
www.state.gov/www/about_state/schools
Office of Overseas Schools
Department of State
Washington, DC 20522-0132
Tel: 202.261.8200
Fax: 202.261.8224
E-mail: OverseasSchools@state.gov

Overseas Teacher's Digest is an on-line magazine devoted to the
interests and concerns of teachers overseas, with member forums and
links to various sites of interest. It features a searchable database of
past issues.
http://overseasdigest.com

Pimsleur Language Tapes are available in 27 languages, and the
company also offers other materials for learning foreign languages.
www.languagetapes.com/index.html

Reliance National Insurance is one of the world's largest
providers of medical insurance for people living overseas.
www.reliancenational.com
Reliance National Insurance
77 Water Street
New York, NY 10005
Tel: 212.858.3600
Fax: 212.858.3612

Relocation Central provides relocation information and features
links to medical, housing, and other expatriate assistance services all
over the world.
www.relocationcentral.com/international/Welcome.html

Applications for **Rotary's Ambassadorial Scholarships** are available from most Rotary Clubs. Listings can be found in your local telephone directory.
www.rotary.org/programs/amb_scho/index.htm
Rotary International
One Rotary Center
1560 Sherman Avenue
Evanston, IL 60201
Tel: 847.866.3000
Fax: 847.328.8554

Settler International provides relocation services, plus destination handbooks giving general information on things such as housing, schools, transportation, insurance, etc. for 10 countries. It has 26 offices worldwide.
www.settler-international.com/index.html

Student Exchange Net provides a broad overview of exchange organizations, information about agencies involved in cultural and academic exchanges, and other resources.
www.studentexchange.net

Tales from a Small Planet is a literary and humor magazine for expatriates, with links to various expatriate services and message boards.
www.talesmag.com

The United States Customs Bureau
www.customs.ustreas.gov
Customs Headquarters
1300 Pennsylvania Avenue N.W.
Room 6.3D
Washington, DC 20229

The United States Distance Learning Association features links to dozens of sites with information about all aspects of distance learning, from pre-kindergarten to post graduate.
www.usdla.org

The University of Phoenix is the world's largest "on-line" university, offering undergraduate, certificate, and graduate degrees in a wide variety of disciplines.
www.phoenix.edu/index_flat.html
The University of Phoenix
Tel: (Toll-free in the U.S.) 800.773.2918

The University of Texas "Telecampus" offers on-line courses and programs K-12 through post-graduate.
www.telecampus.utsystem.edu
The University of Texas TeleCampus
Tel: (Toll-free in the U.S.) 888.839.2716
E-mail: telecampus@utsystem.edu

Vacation Homes Unlimited, a home exchange company operating since 1986, has listings in 40 different countries.
www.vacation-homes.com
Vacation Homes Unlimited
16654 Soledad Canyon Road, Suite 214
Santa Clarita, CA 91351
Tel: (Toll-free in the U.S.) 800.848.7927

Voltage Valet provides information about the electrical requirements, plus links to suppliers of electronic products and adapters for use throughout the world.
www.voltagevalet.com/idx.html
Voltage Valet Division, Hybrinetics, Inc.
225 Sutton Place
Santa Rosa, California 95407
Tel: (Toll-free in the U.S.) 800.247.6900
Tel: (International) +707.585.0333
Fax: 707.585.7313

NOTES

About *Echo Valley*

Terry Harris is not the real name of the publisher of *Echo Valley*, and the name of his publishing company, its principals, and other details have been changed in this book for obvious reasons. Shortly after our return from Prague, after I threatened litigation, all rights to *Echo Valley* reverted to me. Reliable sources inform me that Terry Harris is now a taxi driver. (True!) The book is currently out of print.

About the Czech language

Czech is a Slavic language, using—as does English—the Roman alphabet. However, the language uses various accent marks that are essential to proper pronunciation and understanding. These marks don't appear in the text, which, while it will certainly offend purists, made the typesetter's job a lot easier. We hope that this doesn't interfere with your enjoyment of the book.

ACKNOWLEDGEMENTS

I wish to thank, above all, my wife and children for being the remarkable, adventuresome, and resilient people they are. Together, we managed in our own small way to conquer the world.

My deepest gratitude extends also to Eva Kacerová, our guardian angel, for her kindness, generosity, and good humor throughout our stay in Prague, and for her continued friendship now; to Dr. James Regan of the U.S.C. MPW program for introducing me to Eva; to Pastor Jim and Peggy Krikava for the friendship and encouragement they and their children extended to all of us; to Steve and Leslie Malott, who helped make a foreign place feel like home; to Michael and Young Joo Paprok for their insights and continued friendship; and to Nancy and Jaroslav Najman for the many enjoyable excursions and their friendship.

Correspondence with various people—some of which appears in the book—was a source of incalculable comfort, reassurance, and humor—and also provided an invaluable record of our journey. I'd like to thank J. B. White for keeping a martini glass chilled for me; Scott White for his astute literary criticism and facile wit; Jim Lashly for his encouragement and support during bleak times; Andrew Behar for keeping me employed and amused; Sara Sackner for her understanding, encouragement, and wit; Cynthia Kear for her theories and commiseration; and Barbara Morgenroth for her encouragement and boundless energy.

Thanks also to James T. Webb of Great Potential Press, whose interest in my family's adventure in Prague ultimately led to publication of this book, and to Lynn Gudhus, whose editorial suggestions and input improved the book immeasurably.

Many people contributed to this book by answering an Internet-based questionnaire. Their wisdom and thoughtful responses provided ideas and insight that helped give greater perspective to all aspects of the book. I'd like to thank Caryn Bunshaft, Camilla Lofving, David Howard, Cecilia Ortiz, Colin Bruce, Danielle Surkatty, David Cook, Donald R. Reid, J. R. Coley, Kage Glantz, Karlos Knapp, Lisa Mann, Pam Petrillo, Peter Croft, and Terry Zlabinger.

In addition, I'd like to thank Carmen Quiran at KLM Cargo in San Francisco; Monique Dollonne of International Studies and Cultural Specialists, Inc.; Jacques Pinault; Jean-Claude and Brigitte Lagoutte; and Jean-Baptiste and Myriam Hoffmann.

INDEX

A

B